THE GENDER TRAP

A CLOSER LOOK AT SEX ROLES

Carol Adams & Rae Laurikietis

Cartoons by Andy Johnson

Virago

in association with Quartet Books London

First published by VIRAGO Ltd 1976
in association with Quartet Books Ltd
27 Goodge Street, London W1P 1FD

ISBN 0 704 32803 8 Casebound Edition
ISBN 0 704 33801 7   Paperback Edition

Printed in Great Britain by litho by The Anchor Press Ltd
and bound by Wm Brendon & Son Ltd
both of Tiptree, Essex

THE GENDER TRAP

BOOK 1: Education and Work
BOOK 2: Sex and Marriage
BOOK 3: Messages and Images

THE GENDER TRAP is a series of books about the sex roles imposed on girls and boys in our society, written for young people in school, college and at work, and for their teachers and parents.

Book 1: *EDUCATION AND WORK* looks at our upbringing, education and work. It discusses sex roles in the family and at school, and shows how choices for girls, especially, are narrowed down as their 'feminine' role is gradually imposed, and how because of lack of opportunities, girls often go into unskilled and unsatisfying work. Housework and what it means in the lives of women is discussed as are trade unions, the Equal Pay Act and the Anti-Discrimination Bill. Hard facts and provocative questions together encourage girls and boys to see how rigid notions of 'femininity' and 'masculinity' in areas of education and work can restrict both sexes. The next two books, to be published shortly, also in hard- and paperback editions, complete the series. Each book includes cartoons, poems, stories, extracts, interviews, questions, ideas for projects, discussion and debate. *THE GENDER TRAP* is both an essential handbook for use in schools and colleges, and a comprehensive introduction to these crucial issues for the general public.

Carol Adams and Rae Laurikietis are both in their mid-twenties, and both are history graduates. They teach history/social studies and English respectively at a London comprehensive school.

VIRAGO is a feminist publishing imprint: 'It is only when women start to organize in large numbers that we become a political force, and begin to move towards the possibility of a truly democratic society in which every human being can be brave, responsible, thinking and diligent in the struggle to live at once freely and unselfishly.'

SHEILA ROWBOTHAM, *Women, Resistance and Revolution*

CONTENTS

AUTHORS' NOTE

In the last few years the subject of Women's Liberation has become a major issue. People ask what it is that women want liberating from, for what, and to do what in the future?

This series of books, intended for young people in schools, colleges and at work, and for their teachers, attempts to answer some of the many questions behind these larger ones. What emerges is that Women's Liberation is not a cause on its own for the benefit of women only. Rather it is part of a larger movement which asks both men and women to question their accepted roles in society.

This first book looks at how children are brought up and educated, and at the world of housework, work and trade unions. The second book examines the relationship between the sexes, love, marriage, and the family. The third book deals with the messages and images we receive from our language, humour, and the mass media.

As a whole *The Gender Trap* shows how unjust and restrictive a society is that programmes its men and women to lead separate and different lives according to stereotypes, and suggests that things could be different.

C.A. and R.L. 1975

ACKNOWLEDGEMENTS

We should like to thank the following for permission to quote from their work: Peggy Seeger for 'I'm Gonna be an Engineer'; Glenys Lobban for the information on children's roles; Scott Foresman for permission to quote from their *Guidelines for Improving the Image of Women in Textbooks*; Margherita Rendel for the information about job applications; Maureen Colquhoun, M.P., for talking to us about women in Parliament; Shirley Moreno for her 'Story', reprinted from the *Women's Liberation Review*, Vol. 1, October 1972; *Shrew* for their 'Poem'; Leonora Lloyd, from whose pamphlet *Women Workers in Britain* we quote often in this book; and May Hobbs for talking to us about the Night Cleaners' Action Campaign.

Finally, we should like to thank the many people – too many to list here – who have advised and encouraged us with our work and research for this book.

UNIT ONE:

THE BEST YEARS OF YOUR LIFE

RECIPE

TAKE

**One newly born baby –
any race, any colour**

Find out what sex it is

THEN

Before they realize what's happening

Dress her in pink	Dress him in blue
Give her Barbie Doll	Give him Action Man
Teach her about 'femininity'	Teach him about 'masculinity'
Don't expect too much of her	Expect a hell of a lot of him
Protect her	Make him protect himself
Encourage her incompetence	Encourage his confidence
At school, instruct her in domesticity	At school, train him to earn a living

Do this, and a lot more, all through their lives: make them feel different. And the result?

A 'real' woman   A 'real' man

WHAT HAVE THEY GOT IN COMMON?

UNIT ONE:
THE BEST YEARS OF YOUR LIFE

13

I'M GONNA BE AN ENGINEER

© CONSTRUCTED by PEGGY SEEGER

EASILY

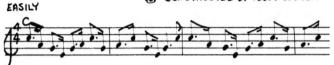

When I was a lit-tle girl I wished I was a boy, I tagged a-long be-hind the gang & wore my

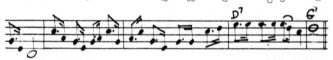

cor-dur-oys, Every-body said I on-ly did it to an-noy, But I was gon-na be an en-gi-neer.

MOM-MA told me "can't you be a LA-DY? YOUR DU-TY IS TO MAKE ME THE MOTH-ER OF A PEARL

WAIT UN-TIL YOU'RE OLD-ER, DEAR, AND MAY-BE YOU'LL BE GLAD THAT YOU'RE A GIRL."

(this part only after verses 1, 3, 5, + 7)

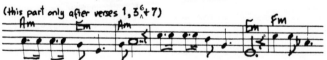

DAIN-TY AS A DRES-DEN STA-TUE, GEN-TLE AS A JER-SEY COW; SMOOTH AS SILK,

GIVES CREAM-Y MILK: LEARN TO COO, LEARN TO MOO, That's what to do to be a la-dy now.

NOTE: the words take some fitting into the above skeletal tune - but if not sung too fast the song sings well.

15

2

When I went to school I learned to write
    and how to read,
Some history, geography and home
    economy,
And typing is a skill that every girl is sure
    to need,
To while away the extra time until the time
    to breed,
And then they had the nerve to say,
    'What would you like to be?'
I says, 'I'm gonna be an engineer!'

NO, YOU ONLY NEED TO LEARN
    TO BE A LADY
THE DUTY ISN'T YOURS, FOR TO
    TRY AND RUN THE WORLD,
AN ENGINEER COULD NEVER
    HAVE A BABY,
REMEMBER, DEAR, THAT YOU'RE
    A GIRL.

3

So I become a typist and I study on the sly,
Working out the day and night so I can
    qualify,
And every time the boss come in,
    he pinched me on the thigh,
Says, 'I've never had an engineer!'

YOU OWE IT TO THE JOB TO BE A
    LADY,
IT'S THE DUTY OF THE STAFF
    FOR TO GIVE THE BOSS A WHIRL,
THE WAGES THAT YOU GET ARE
    CRUMMY, MAYBE,
BUT IT'S ALL YOU GET, 'CAUSE
    YOU'RE A GIRL.

She's smart! (for a woman)
I wonder how she got that way?
You get no choice
You get no voice
Just stay mum,
Pretend you're dumb,
That's how you come to be a lady today!

4

Then Jimmy come along and we set up a
    conjugation,
We were busy every night with loving
    recreation,
I spent my days at work so he could get
    his education,
And now he's an engineer!

HE SAYS, 'I KNOW YOU'LL ALWAYS
    BE A LADY,
IT'S THE DUTY OF MY DARLING
    TO LOVE ME ALL HER LIFE,
COULD AN ENGINEER LOOK
    AFTER OR OBEY ME?
REMEMBER, DEAR, THAT YOU'RE
    MY WIFE!'

5

As soon as Jimmy got a job, I studied hard
    again,
Then, busy at me turret-lathe a year or
    so, and then,
The morning that the twins were born,
    Jimmy says to them,
'Kids, your mother was an engineer!'

YOU OWE IT TO THE KIDS TO BE
    A LADY,
DAINTY AS A DISH-RAG,
    FAITHFUL AS A CHOW,
STAY AT HOME; YOU GOT TO
    MIND THE BABY,
REMEMBER YOU'RE A MOTHER
    NOW.

6

Every time I turn around there's something
    else to do,
Cook a meal or mend a sock or sweep a
    floor or two,
Listen in to Jimmy Young - it makes me
    want to spew
I WAS GONNA BE AN ENGINEER!

I REALLY WISH THAT I COULD
    BE A LADY,
I COULD DO THE LOVELY THINGS
    THAT A LADY'S S'POSED TO DO,
I WOULDN'T EVEN MIND IF ONLY
    THEY WOULD PAY ME,
AND I COULD BE A PERSON TOO.

What price - for a woman?
You can buy her for a ring of gold;
To love and obey
(Without any pay)
You get a cook or a nurse
For better or worse
You don't need a purse when a lady
    is sold!

7

But now that times are harder, and my
    Jimmy's got the sack,
I went down to Vickers, they were glad to
    have me back,
I'm a third-class citizen, my wages tell me
    that,
But I'm a first-class engineer!

THE BOSS HE SAYS, 'I PAY YOU AS
    A LADY,
YOU ONLY GOT THE JOB 'CAUSE I
    CAN'T AFFORD A MAN,
WITH YOU I KEEP THE PROFITS
    HIGH AS MAY BE
YOU'RE JUST A CHEAPER PAIR OF
    HANDS!'

You got one fault! You're a woman.
You're not worth the equal pay,
A bitch or a tart,
You're nothing but heart,
Shallow and vain,
You got no brain,
Go down the drain like a lady today!

I BEEN A SUCKER EVER SINCE I
  WAS A BABY,
AS A DAUGHTER, AS A WIFE, AS A
  MOTHER, AND A DEAR –
BUT I'LL FIGHT THEM AS A
  WOMAN, NOT A LADY,
I'LL FIGHT THEM AS AN
  ENGINEER!

8

I listened to my mother and I joined a
  typing pool,
I listened to my lover and I sent him
  through his school,
If I listen to the boss, I'm just a bloody
  fool,
And an underpaid engineer!

Why doesn't the woman in the song want to be a lady?
Why is it so hard for her to become an engineer?
How much truth do you think there is in the song?
Could it apply to you?

17

1
'I'M GONNA BE
AN ENGINEER'

Almost from the moment you are born you are taught how to be a male, or how to be a female. Most of the behaviour you probably took to be 'natural' for your sex is really a way of acting and behaving that you have been taught – by your parents, relatives, teachers and all the other adults you meet. You even help each other learn what is supposed to be the 'right' way for a boy or girl to act.

You were taught the difference in all sorts of ways; some are obvious and hard to miss, others are not so obvious. But you were taught, nevertheless, that being a boy is one thing, being a girl is another. This is what is meant by sex-role stereotyping.

This book is intended to make you more aware of what is going on around you to make you the sort of person that you are. So, if you do just happen to have been born a boy, perhaps things in general do not seem to be too bad – that is, until you take a closer look. If, on the other hand, you just happen to have been born a girl, you might already have noticed a few instances when things seemed just a little unfair. And perhaps you wondered why.

Suppose, just suppose, you are a girl who wants to be an engineer. The song is a good introduction to what some of this book is about – just what is it that is stopping girls from being engineers, or anything else for that matter? Can you really decide what you want to do, what kind of person you want to be? Or is it decided for you by the 'messages' you receive from all around you? Are you expected to stand up for yourself, make decisions for yourself and eventually support yourself? Or are you taught to 'act like a lady' at the expense of what you really want, or to 'act like a man' when you would rather be gentle and affectionate?

There is one major biological difference between men and women about which no one would argue – sexually men and women have different functions. However, this one difference has led to the idea that, not only are the bodies different, but the personalities and roles in life of the two sexes are different too. So different in fact that this has led to various myths about men and women:

Myth number one Females are passive and unaggressive.
They care for and support others.
They are domestic and dependent.
They are easily upset and emotional, given to crying.
They should be dominated by men.

Myth number two Males are active and aggressive, independent and adventurous.
They can cope with the world.
They are logical and unemotional.
They ought to be able to dominate women.
They are tough, violent, ambitious, ruthless.

Myth number three If males don't behave in a masculine way and females in a feminine way there is something wrong with them.

People are brought up to believe that these myths are true. If men and women do act out these beliefs they damage not only themselves but each other. Men often fail to live up to what they think is expected of them. Women have so little expected of them that they rarely reach their full capacities. As men and women are taught to be so different it becomes very hard for them to get on together and actually to see each other as equals. Here is a list of the qualities that are generally accepted as male and female:

Male	Female
hard	soft
tough	gentle
brutal	kind
cold	affectionate
brave	timid
assertive	quiet
strong	weak
unemotional	emotional

This is a list of opposite qualities – the male and female stereotypes. If these stereotypes could be broken down, then men and women could be on an equal footing – somewhere in the middle.

Have you ever admired a man for being tough and brutal?
Or a woman for being quiet and meek?
What qualities do the people you admire have?
Do you see some of the people you know as being more masculine or more feminine than others?
How do you see yourself in this respect?

2
IN THE
BEGINNING

Parents, or discrimination starts in the pram

It has been estimated that if all women could choose the sex of their babies, the world would be vastly over-populated by men.

Baby boys are generally more popular than baby girls. Some people go on 'trying' for a boy, but end up with 'only' a family of girls. Boys are expected to weigh more at birth than girls. It's rumoured that women know if they are going to have a boy because they 'kick' more before birth.

Once born, the baby's sex starts to be of extraordinary importance. Parents will go to great lengths to distinguish the sex of their babies so that friends and outsiders do not make a mistake. Baby girls are dressed in pink and have their bedrooms decorated in suitably feminine colours. Boys are dressed in blue, their clothes are plain and practical. Their rooms are given the appropriate manly symbols – boats on the wallpaper rather than roses. There's rarely a chance of mistaking a boy's room for a girl's room – parents have seen to that.

From an early age restrictions arise – girls are discouraged from being 'messy' and dirtying their pretty clothes. But 'boys will be boys', and it is expected that they will be more adventurous and exploratory and get dirty in the process. In the advertisements for soap powders it's invariably the boys who come home dirty; thus the image is kept going even if it's not always true to life.

The next time someone you know has a baby, notice for yourself how they treat the child, and what preparations they have made for it. Do you get embarrassed if you have mistaken the sex of someone's baby?

Mother of a four-year-old:
'I'll have to get David's hair cut for him soon –
otherwise people will be mistaking him for a girl.'

As children grow older, the differences remain in the way they are treated by parents and adults, and this does one thing – it makes sure that boys and girls conform to the 'proper' behaviour for their sex.

This putting across of sex roles happens in many sorts of situation. Imagine a family: mother, father and a young boy and girl of roughly the same age. What do you think would happen in the following situations:

Out for a walk – a building is being demolished. To whom does the father point out the more complicated points of the job, his son or his daughter?

They pass a baby in a pram – is the daughter expected to be more interested than the son?

A fire engine rushes past the house. Who is called to the window to watch, the boy or the girl?

The mother is given flowers. Whom does she ask to arrange them for her – son or daughter?

Which child is assumed to be more interested in a wedding, or in the contents of a shop window – the boy or the girl?

Relatives visit the family – which child do you think they kiss and compliment on looking nice, and which do they shake hands with and make remarks about growing stronger?

The same applies to the language used to children. Which of these words and phrases would you use to a boy and which to a girl?

Be a man	A good sport
Boys will be boys	A little angel
Act like a lady	As good as gold
A little devil	A right tearaway
As pretty as a picture	A brave lad
Bossy	Cry-baby
A big sissy	A tomboy
Cute	Sensitive
How sweet!	Aren't you adorable!

How did parents and friends talk about you when you were little?

Would you bring up your children at all differently from the way you were brought up?

Would you treat a son in the same way as a daughter?

3
'BOYS FIX THINGS, GIRLS NEED THINGS FIXED'

Toys and games

Children are given toys according to their sex. This would not matter much if the point of playing with toys was simply to amuse oneself – but there is more to it than that. Playing is important – it teaches skills and patterns of behaviour.

Look at the toys labelled 'suitable for girls': on the whole, they represent in miniature what the girl can expect later on in life – sewing sets, cookers, tea sets, dolls and prams. These tend to teach skills that are quiet and domestic. They also prepare girls for their expected roles of wives and mothers.

The toys aimed at boys reflect quite a different world and teach a different set of skills: trains, cars, guns, model planes, Meccano and construction sets, and so on. Whatever they are, they demand more thought and action. Boys want to know how they work. Being given these toys encourages behaviour that is inquiring, adventurous and aggressive – like running, fighting and competing.

Even if a child is given a bicycle, there is still a distinction made between models for girls and models for boys. Without a crossbar, the design of a girl's bike is structurally less sound than that of a boy. Why is it that a boy will demand an Action Man, while the girl is content with a Barbie Doll – which just needs to be kept looking nice?

What happens if a girl asks for a model car or a woodworking set? Or if a boy asks for a doll to play with? Are adults likely to discourage them from playing with toys regarded as unsuitable for their sex? Do they react as if it is something quite unusual – even a little unnatural – and hastily make more suitable sugges-

25

tions? Even toys have to be freed from their connections with one sex or the other. Toys are toys, so why not choose them on the basis that they are worth playing with, rather than because they are suitable for your sex?

To avoid all this, from the earliest possible age children need to be exposed to playthings of the widest possible variety.

If you examine the games children play among themselves you will often see them acting out adult roles.

Take girls playing together – they are preparing early for a female role. They are in the Wendy house, playing school, dressing up in old clothes, having tea parties. They have learned early what girls are supposed to do.

When boys play together, the games are often active and involve a great deal more physical movement: tree-climbing, building, cowboys and Indians, spacemen, cops and robbers and so on. Girls are excluded for the simple reason that it is assumed they cannot keep up. Early on little boys have started to get a low opinion of the abilities of little girls. Even where they do play together, the girls often take orders from the boys, or the games break up into the acting out of adult behaviour. In 'doctors' for example, the boys are the doctors, the girls are the nurses.

What games did you play when you were younger that involved the other sex?

Did the boys allow the girls along as a favour, or grudgingly, on condition that they would keep up?

How often did one sex leave out the other from the games that were being played?

Divide the following list of toys into those usually given to girls and those usually given to boys:

railway set	toy soldiers	Lego
doll's house	train set	cowboy/Indian outfit
skipping rope	Meccano	doll's pram
conkers	boxing gloves	air gun, pistol

model aeroplane	chemistry set	kite
darts	beads	model microscope
nurse's uniform	makeup set	stencil set
Action Man	tea set	Barbie Doll
Sting Ray	Hot Wheels	

Do you think both sexes come out equally in the toy department
– or does one come out better than the other?

Is there any reason why there should be a difference between
what a young girl and her brother get?

What are your own ideas concerning what are suitable toys for
girls and boys?

Your younger brother insists on taking a rag-doll to bed with
him. What is your reaction? Your parents' reaction?

Your younger sister wants you to build her a go-kart. Do you
think it is a good idea for her to have one?

Would you buy a boy a doll, a toy oven or a nurse's uniform for
his birthday? What reasons would you give for your decision?

Why is it usually boys who are given guns and rifles? Does this
encourage 'masculine' behaviour?

What is your definition of a 'tomboy' or a 'sissy'? Were you ever
accused of being one or the other? How did you feel about it?
Did this affect how you behaved later on at all?

The following dialogue is taken from a cartoon strip. It shows
Margaret, Tommy and Dennis, three schoolchildren, having an
argument in the park. This is how it goes:

DENNIS: The trouble with you, Margaret, is you think ya
know *everything*.

MARGARET: I know a lot of things *you* don't know!

DENNIS: Well, I know something *you* don't know!

MARGARET: What's that?

DENNIS: I know you don't know as much as ya *think* ya
know! Don't pay no attention to Margaret,
Tommy, she's a *dumb-bell*!

MARGARET: Well, you're an *addle-brained imbecile*!

DENNIS: Oh, yeah? Well you're a bone-head!

MARGARET: And you're a *dim-witted dolt*!

DENNIS: What the heck's a dolt?

MARGARET: If you *weren't* one, you'd *know*!

DENNIS: You're a dopey *numskull*!

MARGARET: You're a *brainless, idiotic incompetent*!

DENNIS: Yeah? Well, you're a . . . a . . .

MARGARET: You can't get the best of me, Dennis, I know too many words!

DENNIS: Well, you're even worse than all them things you said *I was*!

MARGARET: Oh? And what could possibly be worse than *those* things?

DENNIS: You're a . . . a . . .

MARGARET: I'm waiting. Go ahead, what am I?

DENNIS: YOU'RE A . . . A . . . GIRL!!

TOMMY: Boy! You sure told *her*!

DENNIS: Yeah. With all her big words she can't top THAT!

from *Dennis the Menace* by HART KETCHAM

Presumably the author intended this to be firstly funny, and also, possibly, to reflect some truth about the world.

Did you find it funny?

Have you ever heard an argument between children along those lines?

Margaret seemed to have the edge over Dennis for almost the whole of the argument. But how did he completely defeat her?

What did Tommy mean when he said, 'With all her big words she can't top THAT!'?

How many of the people you know wish they had been born the opposite sex? Do they say why?

Have you ever gone through this phase?

4
WHAT DID YOU LEARN IN SCHOOL TODAY?

WHAT DID YOU LEARN IN SCHOOL TODAY,
DEAR LITTLE GIRL OF MINE?

I learned how to cook and sew,
I learned that's all girls need to know.
I learned that men go up in space,
That man is the word for the human race.
That's what I learned in school today,
That's what I learned in school.

Here is an example of what girls actually learn in school: these
are some questions taken from the C.S.E. Housecraft Papers:

**Your brother and his friend are arriving home for break-
fast, after walking all night on a sponsored walk.
Iron his shirt, that you have previously washed, and press
a pair of trousers ready for him to change into.
Cook and serve a substantial breakfast for them, including toast. Lay the table ready for the meal.
Make your mother and yourself a midday salad meal,
with a cold sweet to follow.**

(1973)

Describe how to clean the following: i) a non-stick frying pan; ii) an ovenware glass casserole; iii) a thermoplastic (Marley) tiled floor; iv) a vinyl-covered floor; v) a lavatory pan.

(1974)

You and your husband are going to spend a weekend with your parents.
Launder a selection of your own and your husband's clothes; these should include a variety of fabrics and finishes. Name these fabrics with labels, when displaying your finished work.
Prepare a meatless evening meal for the two of you, using up left-over cooked vegetables and stale bread.

(1974)

What skills are these girls learning?

Do boys need to know how to do these things?

What sort of practical skills will a boy be likely to have when he leaves school?

From primary days on, school plays an increasingly important part in sex-role stereotyping. Even if, at the end of your school career, you think you can say with complete certainty that 'I never learned a thing at school', or 'I've forgotten everything I was ever taught' you will be wrong. This might be true of subjects, but not of those things you are taught without being fully aware that you are learning them: what you are taught in school, and what you cannot easily unlearn, is that males and females are different and unequal.

You may object to this and say, but surely everyone – boy or girl – is treated the same at school? On the surface there doesn't seem to be any immediately obvious difference. But if you look more closely at what you are taught and who teaches you, at what is expected of you, or at what you are discouraged from doing, you will begin to see that there are differences.

And once you see them, you are in a better position to do something about them.

In your school, in the practical subjects, are girls kept mainly to needlework and home economics, and boys to woodwork, metalwork and technical drawing? If this is so, have you ever asked why?

In some schools boys are encouraged to do *some* needlework and girls to do *a little* metalwork, but is it to the same extent?

Have you ever wanted to take a subject at school but weren't allowed to because of your sex? Was there anything you could do about it?

The organization of your school

'Schools are, at least partly, responsible for the beliefs common amongst girls that training is unimportant, their jobs are inessential and their husbands are financially responsible for them. Poor job opportunities, low pay and discrimination at work both cause and reflect discrimination at school . . .

'The education system is, we believe, creating discriminatory attitudes and low expectations in new generations of children.'

From the National Council for Civil Liberties
Women's Rights, November 1973

Schools play a large part in convincing girls that their education is not really important. One way to keep alive the idea that males and females are different is to educate them separately in single-sex schools. The results of this separate-but-equal arrangement of education are not very encouraging. Most girls' schools have poorer facilities for the sciences than boys' schools. Obviously, these schools will produce fewer scientists. Girls at mixed schools usually have access to better science equipment. The gap between girls and boys in their achievement in science widens as they move through school. But in mixed schools the gap is not so wide.

On the other hand, there is a strong case for saying that girls do better, in general, in an all-girls school, where they are not likely to feel outdone by the boys. In this situation their achievement often tends to be in the so-called 'girls'' subjects – languages and the arts.

Even if you go to a mixed school, the girls are still separated from the boys by various devices. In some schools you will find these situations:

The register: boys' and girls' names in separate lists with the boys first.

Lining up: schoolchildren are so used to being told to line up according to sex, in the playground and outside classrooms, that even when they are given no specific instructions they still do it.

Competition: group work; for the teacher the simple way out is to say 'boys against girls'. Competition is encouraged along sex lines partly because boys often hate the idea of having girls on their side, and vice versa.

Uniform: the girls' uniform is always a skirt, never trousers. Even female teachers are discouraged from wearing trousers by many education authorities. Imagine how much your freedom of movement is restricted by having to wear a skirt.

School rules: among them are restrictions as to length of hair – especially directed against the boys. The less they look like girls the better, presumably.

Separate playgrounds: so that delicate girls can be protected from rough boys. Or, in mixed playgrounds, boys take over while girls stand in small groups around the edge.

Separate gymnasia: one for each sex is a common feature of large schools. Girls dance and do 'keep fit' exercises in theirs, while the boys play volley-ball or something equally strenuous in theirs. Often there are no mixed teams, and separate tuition and instructors.

Assemblies: girls sit, while boys stand – presumably training them for their future role as protectors of the weaker sex. Or if the whole assembly is allowed to sit, then it's the males along one half of the hall, the females along the other.

Outings: how many of them are 'girls only' or 'boys only', with the girls being take round the local nursery, while the boys visit the steelworks?

Look around your school, or think back to when you were there. Chances are that the teachers and staff were separated along sex lines in the jobs done.

Does the following pattern hold true of your school?
Head teacher: male
Deputy: male or female
Cleaning staff: female
Kitchen staff: female
'Dinner ladies': female
Schoolkeeper: male
Heads of houses or years: male
Deputy heads of houses or years: female or male
School nurses: female
Clerical staff, typists: female
Heads of the maths, geography, science, woodwork/
    metalwork departments: male
Heads of the needlework and home economics departments:
    female

Do you think it is likely that girls will do better in a single-sex or a mixed school?
It is often said that having girls in a school has a good influence

on the boys. Do you think this is true?
What exactly do girls contribute to a school that boys don't?
How does the presence of boys in a school affect girls?

5
TEACHERS

We are what we are expected to be

Schoolchildren act according to their teachers' expectations of them.

Woodwork lesson:
A boy shows a piece of wood with a badly hammered-in nail to the teacher, who says, 'Take it away and do it properly.' A girl does exactly the same thing, but the teacher says, 'Give it me and I'll do it for you.' Obviously she is not expected to be competent with wood and nails and is therefore never likely to be so.

Even in primary and junior schools, teachers often expect boys and girls to show different *styles* in their work:
– Boys are expected to work on a big scale, to erect massive block structures.
– Girls are expected to work on a small scale, to make little, homely constructions.
– Boys are assumed to want to know *how* things work and to be logical.
– Girls are assumed to want to know how to make things *look nice* and ornamental and to show a disregard for logic.
– Boys are encouraged to explore the environment round them.
– Girls are protected from it.

School outing:
A group of school children are watching clouds gathering on the horizon.
Boys remark: 'Oh, how pretty!'
Girls inquire: 'Are those cumulus or cirrus clouds?'
Teacher looks surprised – why?

And when you got to secondary school, what about the teachers there? Were you ever taught domestic science by a man? Did you ever come across a male librarian, a female woodwork teacher? If not, no wonder we get the idea that there are 'male' and 'female' subjects. Did the female teachers have trouble with projectors and plugs? Did they call in men for help? Did they say they were no good at maths? They can hardly be expected to encourage their girl students to do things that they have got by without knowing.

Consider whether boys and girls were expected to behave differently in class; if boys were expected to carry heavy materials and girls to make tea. Were girls expected to be more polite than boys?

Think about responding in lessons. Were boys expected to be more questioning and logical, and girls to be docile, diligent, unquestioning? Were girls expected to dress more neatly than boys, to keep their books and desks tidier while boys were allowed to be scruffy? Many boys and girls think they are treated differently for misbehaving – that boys always get blamed for fights even when girls started them, while a higher standard of behaviour is expected of girls. Think carefully about these ways in which teachers, often without realizing it, make distinctions between girls and boys.

Girls and boys are often punished in different ways. Boys get caned far more than girls, and they are treated in a rougher way than a girl would be. Do you think this is fair? Should boys demand the same treatment as girls get? Teachers often expect boys to be chivalrous, opening doors and letting the girls leave first. You may have noticed that teachers tend to compliment girls on their clothes and looks, but will be more likely to praise a boy for his playing in a match. What makes pupils popular with teachers? Is it the same for both sexes?

Teachers often use phrases like:
'Can I have two strong lads to help me . . .'
'I want a sensible girl to . . .'
'Be a gentleman and open the door . . .'
'What language from a lady . . .'

6
READING

Once upon a time – fairy stories

When you were young you read nursery rhymes and fairy stories, or had them read to you. Probably you never thought further about the 'hidden messages' they contained, some of which were:

– Lovely maidens and princesses usually have to wait passively for some prince to come along.
– All other females are ugly hags, witches or stepmothers (invariably wicked).
– None of the females do anything worthwhile.
– Happy endings are those in which the couple 'got married and lived happily ever after'.
– Men do the rescuing and the brainwork. They are independent, brave and given to overcoming insurmountable difficulties.
– The most important decision a woman can make is – who her future husband is going to be.
– Beauty equals success which equals marriage.
– Women are rarely friends with each other – they compete.
– Women can rarely change their own lives – they have to wait for men to do it for them.

Have you ever heard of an ugly stepfather or a brave princess rescuing a poor, lonely prince? In fact, can you remember *any* fairy stories in which the women weren't getting a raw deal, one way or another?
What were the fairy stories and folk tales you heard or read as a child? Make a list of them, then compare the male and female

characters. How are the females portrayed?

Try to write a fairy story that doesn't have the sexist content of the stories you were taught. For instance, you could have an alternative ending to 'They got married and lived happily ever after'. Or have a female in the main role who did the rescuing and the brainwork. There are many other alternatives.

Early readers

The following chart is an analysis of sex roles in reading schemes widely used in schools for teaching children to read.

THE CHILDREN'S ROLES

	Toys and pets	Activities	Taking the lead in joint activities	Learning a new skill	The adult roles shown
Girls only	1. Doll 2. Skipping rope 3. Doll's pram	1. Preparing the tea 2. Playing with dolls 3. Taking care of younger siblings	1. Hopping 2. Shopping with parents 3. Skipping	1. Taking care of younger siblings	1. Mother 2. Aunt 3. Grandmother
Boys only	1. Car 2. Train 3. Aeroplane 4. Boat 5. Football	1. Playing with cars 2. Playing with trains 3. Playing football 4. Lifting or pulling heavy objects 5. Playing cricket 6. Watching adult males in occupational roles 7. Heavy gardening	1. Going exploring alone 2. Climbing trees 3. Building things 4. Taking care of pets 5. Sailing boats 6. Flying kites 7. Washing and polishing Dad's car	1. Taking care of pets 2. Making/building 3. Saving/rescuing people or pets 4. Playing sports	1. Father 2. Uncle 3. Grandfather 4. Postman 5. Farmer 6. Fisherman 7. Shop or business owner 8. Policeman 9. Builder 10. Bus driver 11. Bus conductor 12. Train driver 13. Railway porter

THE CHILDREN'S ROLES

	Toys and pets	Activities	Taking the lead in joint activities	Learning a new skill	The adult roles shown
Both Sexes	1. Book 2. Ball 3. Paints 4. Bucket and spade 5. Dog 6. Cat 7. Shop	1. Playing with pets 2. Writing 3. Reading 4. Going to the seaside 5. Going on a family outing			1. Teacher 2. Shop assistant

from GLENYS LOBBAN, *Forum for the Discussion of New Trends in Education*

What obvious differences do you notice?

Here are some extracts from Ladybird primary school reading books, in which not only the words but the pictures that go with them show a very restricted role for females, and a very different one for males.

'Peter has to help Daddy with the car, Jane has to help Mummy in the house.'
' "Yes," said Peter, "You make the tea and I will draw." '
' "Yes, I will be like Mummy and get the tea," says Jane.'

What picture of 'Mum' do you get here?
Is it true of your Mum?
Do girls always do as boys tell them?

'Peter has the red ball. He plays with the boys with the red ball. Jane looks on.'
'Peter has a punch ball, a toy aeroplane, an electric car, and Jane buys balloons, a skipping rope and a scrapbook.'
' "Mary and I won't play if you fight," says Jane.'

Is it true to life that girls don't fight?
What do you think of their choice of toys?

' "I want to be a big man," says the boy.'
' "I do not want to be so big," says his sister. "I like to be as I am now." '

Do you think the boy will meet any problems if he tries to be a 'big man'?
Will his sister always be so contented?

In another reader, from the 'Through the Rainbow' series, we find:

'When everything was ready, the girls shouted to the boys and they came running into the kitchen for a feast of hot cakes and jam.'

Children who read these books will invariably get the message that boys are better than girls at everything apart from house-work and child care; that the place of women is in the home and that of boys outside it. Girls who want to be engineers are subtly being told that they can't be. And it is never suggested that boys should be doing what girls do.

Where have the children learnt behaviour like this?
Is it good for either of the sexes?
Do you think this sort of writing for children should be changed?

Here are lists of words given in a children's picture dictionary for them to write sentences about their parents:

43

MUMMY	DADDY
pretty, apron, works, cooks,	plays, shows, paddles, watch,
cares, hug, love, always	case, paper, pipe, drives

What does this teach children?

Comics for girls – boarding school and ballet shoes

Another influence on your ideas is that of the comics you read. If you are a girl, then you most likely read one of the many popular girls' comics on the market. The subjects of the stories in girls' comics play their part in presenting girls with a limited world. Any excitement or activity is kept to certain selected areas. Girls have adventures in boarding school or at home. They have 'female' careers in ballet and nursing – they never break out into other parts of the big wide world. Let's take a closer look at some stories in a typical girls' comic.

'Boy Blue . . . the Rockin' Robot' is about a girl who idolizes a pop star: 'Like most girls of her age, Janet Freeman adored pop music and looked forward to every Wednesday evening when Pete Dawson presented his Popular Pop Show.' She is livid with her brother who interferes with the programme with his electrical work: he is making a robot. However, she agrees to make clothes for the robot: 'I'm no good at sewing, Janet – that's a girl's job, and I want you to buy him a wig.' So Janet spends all her money on the wig and gives up going to a pop concert to sew the clothes to keep her brother happy. However, all her sacrifices in being a 'good little housewife' are rewarded when her brother makes the robot sing – now she has her own pop idol . . . lucky Janet!

'Stella at Stage School' is typical of the 'career' stories for girls, in which a poor girl makes good by winning a scholarship to stage school. The dancing life of 'Moira Kent' is along the same lines. She is not only talented, but is a good soul who befriends poor girls and is generally kind to people.

The cartoon characters in the comic are not too flattering for girls. One is 'Toots', who does all the housework while her mother is ill in bed. She does it so badly that Mum has to get up after one day instead of three. The alternative is 'Mighty Mo', the Amazon-type girl, who breaks the kids' swing when she gets on it but redeems herself by making them a huge see-saw. Big girls have their good side.

Notice also the kinds of competition and special offers made to girls. They have to unjumble the letters of a pop star's name, cut out and colour his picture for the 'Fab Four' competition. Free with the comic comes a charming bracelet . . . 'There's a place for your name . . . or your favourite pop star's . . . or anyone you like.'

Comics for boys – action-packed pages

Comics for boys are about bravery, challenge and adventure. Anything can happen to the characters involved, but it is always exciting and out of the ordinary, taking place in far-off countries, or in the past, or in a war. The boys take enormous risks, find themselves in amazing predicaments, which they come out of successfully. There are no girls, or, if they do appear, their part in the story is insignificant. There are also interesting hobbies and features for these sports-loving, adventure-seeking readers.

Let's look at a typical boys' comic. The cover feature, 'The Rivals', is about two popular football teams, Leeds and Liverpool, and gives the latest account of the strong competition between them with several big action shots.

'Captain Hurricane' is about a group of soldiers in the Second World War: 'They fought their way into deepest Germany in spite of fierce opposition. No British force had shown greater courage and determination to achieve victory than the Royal Marine Commando under the inspired leadership of Captain Hercules.' In this story a girl does appear – she is German, speaking broken English, who teaches one of the soldiers to sow potatoes, when he needed to learn how to mend his captain's uniform – useless woman!

'The Trail to Nowhere' takes place 'somewhere in the wilderness of Arizona in 1872, where a wandering trapper is heading for the mysterious nowhere mountains in search of a gold mine. After an amazing adventure in a ruined Aztec city, involving a giant lizard, he finds a route to a lost hoard of Aztec treasure.' Of course, he has to fight swarms of Indians, a 'fight for our doggoned lives', as he says . . . we have to wait until next week to see if he gets there . . . but what's your guess?

If any boy is left with the need for a bit of activity after reading all this, there are plenty of interesting offers going for him. He can win a Meccano Multi Highway kit or send off for Matchbox Superking trucks. Or he can win a Mustang superkit on the Airfix Model Club page. There's certainly no limit to the action in this collection of 'mysterious intrigue, gripping new tales, an incredible hunch', as the stories are described.

Comics are not for real – they are fantasy and exaggeration – but what exactly are they exaggerating? Why are there no boys at ballet school and no girls exploring the Sahara?

Humanized fiction – girls who think and act, boys who feel and care

---

FACTS

80% of writers of children's books are female. Less than 1% of children's books feature heroines as central characters.

Often children's libraries are arranged in separate sections for boys and girls. Even if this is not done, the contents of the books themselves encourage separate tastes and interests, along the same lines as comics. There are fewer books on hobbies for girls than for boys, and there are few aimed at both sexes – it is assumed that there is no common ground of interest.

It has been found that boys will not read stories written for girls, while girls will read stories written for boys. Do you think this would change if girls were allowed a more interesting image in books?

Books for girls '. . . were usually about goody-goodies who never did anything but faint, sing hymns and cry. No matter what happened to those silly heroines, whether their wicked guardian shut them in a dungeon or their embroidery thread tangled, all they did was weep.' That was Louisa May Alcott's idea of girls' books in the nineteenth century. Do you think things have changed – or are girl heroines still incompetent?

Some children's authors have tried to provide an alternative:

'His mother one day said, "Shipmate, I want to see the sea again, I want to get the city smoke out of my lungs, and put the sea salt there instead. I want to fire my old silver pistol again and see the sea waves jump with surprise." '

from MARGARET HABY,
The Man Whose Mother was a Pirate
(for 6- to 10-year-olds), Atheneum

'Little William wants a doll; other boys call him "sissy" and his father brings him a basketball and an electric train. William enjoys them but still he wants a doll. Finally his grandmother buys him a doll. "He needs it," she says to William's father, "to hug and to cradle and to take to the park so that when he's a father like you, he'll know how to take care of his baby . . ." '

from CHARLOTTE ZOLOTOW, *William's Doll*, Harrow

Textbooks

Publishers are becoming slightly more aware of the way in which women are portrayed in books. One company – Scott Foresman – have brought out a booklet called *Guidelines for Improving the Image of Women in Textbooks.* The idea behind this is to combat the sexist attitudes of the past, when women really were regarded as inferior beings.

'Textbooks are sexist if they omit the actions and achievements of women, if they demean women by using patronizing language, or if they show women only in stereotyped roles with less than the full range of human interests, traits and capabilities. Textbooks should treat women as the equals of men.'

Some of the ways in which this can be brought about are suggested:
– Women politicians, artists and scientists should be mentioned as much as men.
– Writing by female authors should be made much more available.
– In maths and English exercises men and women should appear equal, e.g. no more women counting eggs in baskets while men measure the height of skyscrapers.
– Girls and women should not be presented as more fearful of danger, mice, snakes and insects than males.

'Both men and women have much to gain from the elimination of stereotypes. Textbooks which avoid male and female stereotyping will more accurately represent reality, encourage tolerance for individual differences, and allow more freedom for children to discover and express their needs, interests, and abilities.'

7
CLIMBING THE EXAMINATION LADDER

Your achievements at school are measured by the exams you take, since they help to decide your future. At sixteen, in C.S.E. and O levels, girls do marginally better than boys, although boys take many more science subjects than girls. For example, nearly twenty thousand more boys than girls took maths in 1969, but three thousand more girls than boys took arithmetic at C.S.E. The easier option was thought more suitable for girls.

When it comes to staying on for two years in the sixth form, twice as many boys as girls stay on. Boys also take twice as many A levels. This is when the girls start to 'give up' in the examination rat-race. Have girls decided already that there's no point in competing?

CHART I. NUMBERS TAKING PUBLIC
EXAMINATIONS (1971) *

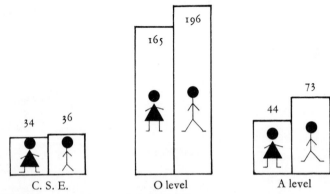

| C. S. E. | O level | A level |

*Figures approximate, in thousands

from *Statistics in Education*, D.E.S., 1971

In a grammar school for girls only, they are more likely to stay on; but they are less likely to do so in a mixed comprehensive. Yet the fact is, that when they do stay on, the pass rate of girls at A level is *higher* than that of boys: 71 per cent as against 67 per cent.

In the sixth form many girls will do non-A level courses – commercial studies, general studies, a few more O levels. While valuable in themselves, these courses are not a stepping-stone to higher education, and are not thought worth taking by boys. Of course, exams aren't everything, but it is boys who are taught to be more exam-orientated.

Another outstanding difference in achievement is in examination subjects chosen by boys and girls. Chart 2 shows an example of the entries for some subjects.

CHART 2. ENTRIES (SUMMER 1971)
ALL BOARDS C.S.E. *

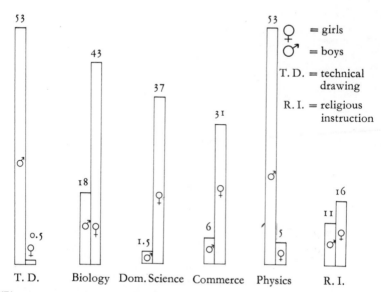

*Figures approximate, in thousands

from *Statistics in Education*, D.E.S., 1971

Results follow the same pattern. Generally boys do better in maths and science and girls in arts and modern languages. Girls get more top grades in the 'female' subjects; they take biology rather than physics if they are 'scientific'. There are some interesting exceptions, however. *Among the few girls who took it, proportionately more girls than boys got the top grade in building and engineering! More boys than girls got top grades in commerce.* So, it seems that when someone genuinely wants to do a subject, they can do well regardless of sex.

The trend is the same at A level, and results show that when girls take science they do just as well as boys. A higher percentage of girls than boys actually pass in all A level subjects.

The higher the level of education, the fewer women are found in it (see chart 3). Most universities accept fewer women than men, and some medical schools limit their quota of women. No wonder fewer girls therefore study science, and it makes the competition for places in arts subjects very intense for girls.

CHART 3. WOMEN IN HIGHER EDUCATION

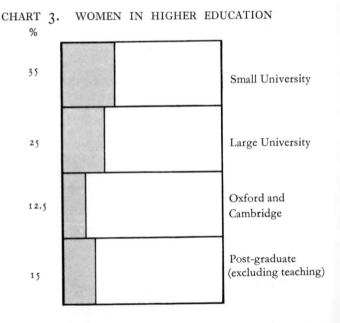

%

35 — Small University

25 — Large University

12.5 — Oxford and Cambridge

15 — Post-graduate (excluding teaching)

CHART 4.   DESTINATIONS ON LEAVING
SCHOOL

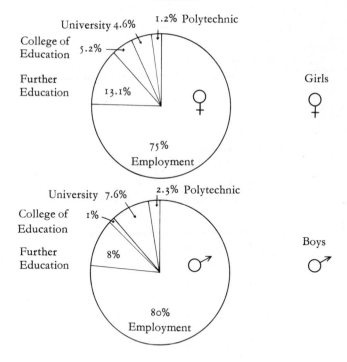

from *Statistics in Education*, D.E.S., 1971

As can be seen from chart 4, many of the girls who are doing as well as the boys at fifteen and sixteen fade out of the education system later, and where they stay they do a more restricted range of subjects. The overall rate for entering for and passing exams is increasing more rapidly for girls than boys, but girls are still far behind.

In these various ways, schools hold girls back from the same achievements and ambitions as boys. There is no such thing as a *free* choice for your future once you have reached the end of your school education – it has already been decided by previous influences and choices. Even if girls go on to higher education the odds are loaded against their finding good jobs.

Why do you think fewer girls than boys take A levels?
Is it because they are less intelligent? Less ambitious? Less competitive?
Is it because they see no point in staying on?
Is it because qualifications are less important for girls?
Is it because there are better things for them to do in life than take exams?
Are boys likely to have a more worthwhile and enjoyable life by passing exams?
When you were asked to choose subjects for the exam courses at school, what influenced your choice?
Would you have chosen different subjects if you were of the opposite sex?
Were you pressured to succeed at school?
Are the pressures greater on boys than on girls?

8
YOUR CHOICE OF CAREER

'Then they had the nerve to say "What would you like to be?" '

Engineer: HIS work as a professional engineer . . .
Company secretary: HE is a key figure in HIS concern.
Cosmetic research: This may appeal to a GIRL interested in science.
Dentistry: Only GIRLS can be trained as dental auxiliaries.
Accountant: The young accountant today, if HE chooses non-graduate training . . .

from *A Careers Guide for School Leavers*

Examine careers books for girls and boys. Are there any differences in the careers suggested? Look also at the pictures. Ever seen a male nurse smiling on the front cover of a nursing handbook, or a G.P.O. ad featuring a smiling postwoman? If a job is presented as *mostly* for the opposite sex, the chances are you will not apply for it. Some jobs and higher-education courses are even trying to recruit more women, but cannot find enough with the right qualifications . . . this situation demands changes in the schools.

Has your education given you an equal chance to get the job you want, to live the life you want?

A survey was carried out by Margherita Rendel of the Institute of Education, applying for jobs advertised in the Sunday newspapers which did not specify sex. Here are some of the replies she got (our italics throughout):

I am afraid the chances are very much *against a woman* being acceptable for the position.

While it is not laid down that the appointment should be a man, in view of the supervisory and committee work involved, I think a *male* applicant would be favoured.

It was not anticipated that this post would be attractive to a woman and on balance I do not think the duties would be *suitable for a woman*.

Many of the replies offered alternative jobs, of inferior status because the applicant was female:

It is unlikely that a woman would be appointed to the post of warden of our centre . . . However, sometime in the future we shall be appointing an *assistant* warden when an application from you would be considered . . .

In spite of the Anti-discrimination Bill, try applying for a job NOT SPECIFIED FOR WOMEN if you are female, and try applying for what is usually considered to be a woman's job if you are male. You will see how rigid the divisions are, how strong the prejudices, and how hard they are to change. It's still unlikely that girls are 'gonna be engineers'.

How often have you heard parents say:
'Education's wasted on a girl . . .'
'A boy must think of his future . . .'
'She'll only get married, so what's the point?'
'A job with prospects, that's what a boy needs.'
'But she's only a girl . . .'

Legal Eag

Market'
Manag
Direct

White Good

The Job—To take ch
the company's make
and execute the str:
profit by the effec
sales statistics and
responsible for th
publicity design,
sales and produ

The Company—
integrated ran
products whic'
their quality.
are set to grow much ι..
next twelve months.

The Man—(He) must be self motivating with a big
head of steam. A sales background is desirable,
but not essential, though he will be experienced
in marketing and sales analysis and familiar with
all forms of commercial advertising. A foreign
language and experience of exporting would be
an advantage. The salary will not be less than
£5,000 and could be substantially higher for the
right
Manag

Write

need
Secretary Bir

Close to Holborn tube station you'll find our bright (when
offices where we're waiting to provide you with a choice o
interesting jobs.

Tell us where your interest lie — and we'll do our best.

If you have previous legal experience, have good shorthand a
like working under a certain amount of pressure and are look
salary of **around £2000**, then we'll introduce you to a senior par
needs an assistant.

If you're interested in finding out the facts behind the headlines th
are several other positions available (S/H or Audio) where yo
directly involved — and be earning a good salary.

We believe that the work we handle is amongst the most
interesting a secretary can do. You'll receive L.V's three
weeks holiday a year and our hours are 9.30 to 5.30.
Why not telephone me. (Staff Manager) and find out
more?

01-242 3826 Ext 59

35

General Manager
Light Engineering   Up to £10,000

This is a unique opportunity for an exceptional man to develop a new
manufacturing project in the Irish Republic.

Aged 33 to 40 (he) will be directly responsible to the President of the
parent company in the U.S.A. for the build-up and management of a
modern, highly-automated plant producing small, engineered
consumer products and employing 100 people.

We seek a qualified Mechanical Engineer, accustomed to direct
practical operational involvement, with at least ten years manufacturing experience in automated light engineering production.
Experience of plastics injection moulding and product development
would be helpful.

Benefits include a company car, non-contributory pension and
assistance with removal expenses.

Which sex do you think the legal eagles are?

59

9
ON THE EDUCATION
OF WOMEN

A sample of sexist quotes

'The glory of a man is knowledge, but the glory of a woman is to renounce knowledge.'

Chinese proverb

'The whole education of women ought to be relative to men. To please them, to be useful to them, to make themselves loved and honoured by them, to educate them when young, to care for them when grown, to counsel them, to console them and to make life sweet and agreeable to them – these are the duties of women at all times and what should be taught them from their infancy.'

from JEAN-JACQUES ROUSSEAU, *Confessions*, Penguin

'Women should receive a higher education, not in order to become doctors, lawyers or professors, but to rear their offspring to be valuable human beings.'

from ALEXIS CARREL, *Man the Unknown*

'We try to educate girls into becoming imitation men and as a result we are wasting and frustrating their qualities of womanhood at a great expense to the community . . . in addition to their needs as individuals our girls should be educated in terms of their main social function – which is to make for themselves, their children and their husbands a secure and suitable home and to be mothers.'

from Newsom Report, *Half Our Future*, H.M.S.O., 1963

'The incentive for girls to equip themselves for marriage and home-making is genetic . . . With the less able girls schools can and should make more adjustments to the fact that marriage looms much larger and nearer in the pupils' eyes than it has ever done before . . . her interest in dress, personal appearance and problems of human relations should be given a central place in her education.'

[But, referring to boys] '. . . At this stage their thoughts turn more often to a career, and only secondly to marriage and the family.'

from Crowther Report, *Fifteen to Eighteen*,
Her Majesty's Stationery Office, 1959

What was your education training you for?

Ten years on

A group of young people in a London school had this to say about their futures:

'In ten years' time I'll be a married man with a couple of kids and a steady job and a house to live in. I would buy a nice big car for the family.'

14-year-old boy

'I'll be a housewife, stuck with the kids' runny noses, two of them, working myself to the bone, sweating over a hot stove, cooking meals all day, getting fatter.'

14-year-old girl

'My ambition is to be a professional footballer and play for Arsenal in front of a full 62,000 crowd and play one of the best games of my life.'

14-year-old boy

'In ten years' time I would like to be working and have a good career. I will be a secretary working for a nice boss.'

15-year-old girl

'I would probably be earning £40–£45 a week as an electrician or mechanic.'

15-year-old boy

'In ten years' time I will be a part-time hairdresser – I will have to be part-time because I will be married with two small children.'

15-year-old girl

UNIT TWO:

THE WORST WORK IS WOMEN'S WORK

WANTED

One able-bodied female needing a job.

QUALIFICATIONS

Not essential, but if educated, commercial or general arts subjects rather than technical training.

MUST BE

Obedient, devoted, addicted to work, self-sacrificing, servile, punctual, reliable, good-humoured, contented, friendly, especially to men, pretty, sexy, thoughtful, able to carry out orders, unambitious, and any other good female qualities would be useful.

CONDITIONS

Long hours, or short hours with extra work at home, unpaid housework on top, low pay, poor working conditions.

THE JOB

Cleaner, shop assistant, waitress, barmaid, nurse, teacher, secretary . . . whichever suits you.

UNIT TWO:
THE WORST
WORK IS WOMEN'S
WORK

8 Women and Trade Unions

'Trade unionists, their wives and families'
The night cleaners – 'working for luxuries'?
Women in action – the background to the
night cleaners' campaign
Fakenham – 'A silly lot of girls'
Equal pay and anti-discrimination
Myths and legends

1
NIGHT TIME. OVERTIME. PART-TIME. ALL THE TIME

> It takes a man to do that job . . . .
> That's women's work . . .
> You couldn't expect a man to . . .
> That's a strange job for a woman . . .
> Jobs for the boys . . .

Expressions like these convey the idea that men and women are expected to do different types of work. This implies that the skills and talents involved are mainly male or mainly female.

Would you be surprised to see a woman unloading a lorry or driving a train? Would you notice if it was a man who did the charring where you work or who looked after the kids at the local nursery?

There is a riddle that goes like this:
A man and his son are driving along.
They have a bad accident.
The boy is taken to hospital.
The surgeon comes out of the operating theatre and says:
'Oh, my God, it's my own son.'
Explain the surgeon's response.
Answer: The surgeon is a woman.

Very few people ever get the answer right – try asking someone yourself.

Men are associated with the really prestigious jobs. Pilots, surgeons, directors, M.P.s are all assumed to be men, unless the prefix 'woman' or 'lady' is attached to it. Considering that women make up 51 per cent of the population, they fill very few of the top jobs (and those that do tend to be very exceptional), and are rarely in positions of power and control.

Men, however, do work that women are protected from doing. The work may be too dangerous, strenuous, or unpleasant, and might involve night work and overtime. If that is the case, then should *men* be doing such work? Why should men have to put up with conditions thought unfit for women? Should men have to accept bad conditions in order to support their wives and families?

The more that work is related to or similar to housework and child care, the less prestige it has and the less money you get for it. If worth is judged by wages alone, anyone would think that the least worthwhile thing to be doing is running a home and looking after children. By these standards the worst work for women, the jobs with no status and low wages, are extensions of the woman's role in her own home: cleaning, cooking, laundry work, shop work, waitressing – all jobs for which little or no training is needed. Even if women do manage to gain qualifications, they almost invariably work in traditionally feminine fields – nursing, teaching, secretarial work. The fact is that no matter what women are doing, it is almost never considered as important or as worthwhile as what men do.

Men's upbringing has taught them to push themselves hard in a competitive world. They are judged on their performance – and on their earnings. They are made to feel less than men if they cannot support a wife and family singlehanded. If they complain about the demands made on them, then it's assumed that they are 'not up to the job'. The qualities that women value in work – companionship, surroundings, etc. (perhaps because their work is so unrewarding?) – men are taught to undervalue.

68

Are most men's jobs more fulfilling than most women's?
What do you think 'fulfilment' involves?
Do you think women value the following more than men:
  companionship and friendliness at work
  pleasant surroundings
  people rather than products
  family life having priority over work?
Would men be more likely than women to go for good wages and prospects in a job?

When you have read this chapter, you may be struck by women's poor record of achievement compared with that of men. Does this show that women are less intelligent, less physically strong, less demanding, less ambitious? Or are they afraid of success? As the saying goes: 'Failure unsexes a man, success a woman.' Women, it would seem, are as afraid of succeeding as men are of failing, because if women are successful it must also mean that they are somehow less 'feminine' than they ought to be. Success and ambition are regarded as proofs of 'masculinity'.

It is often assumed that 'career women' have given up any hope of a happy family life. It is also an accepted idea that women give up a life of their own for the sake of home and family. By upbringing and education, women are not allowed to be themselves, to extend themselves and use their energies and potential. Rather, they are encouraged above all to be of service to someone else: never to themselves. Not that there is anything wrong with being of use to other people – far from it. The point is that women are trained from birth to do this – while men are trained to expect and demand service from women.

But people are starting to question the roles society fits them for and to demand something more. They are demanding more flexibility in the male and female roles, so that toughness and energy are becoming acceptable female qualities, and gentleness and being of service to people acceptable male ones.

How important is it for you to be successful in your career?

What is your idea of a typical 'career woman'?
How would you feel about working for a woman boss?
Which jobs do you think women physically couldn't do?
Are there any jobs that men cannot do because they aren't gentle and tender enough?

2
TRAINING
FOR THE JOB

'Women are a wasted investment'

The education that you get generally leads boys towards a wider and better choice of career than girls. Boys are more likely to leave school with qualifications and to enter a skilled job. But this is not the end of the story. It is the training you get, either immediately before or during the early years of work, that determines your progress – your chances of promotion and higher earnings. Here again, the dice are loaded against women.

FACTS
2 out of 5 full-time further education students are women
1 in 7 day-release students are women
1 in 33 sandwich course students are women

from *Report on Education and
Employment for Women and Girls*,
Association of Teachers in Technical Institutes, 1970

A large number of girls take full-time courses before they start work, but these are usually commercial courses, teaching them the basic office skills that will equip them for jobs as personal assistants or office workers. There is little opportunity for them to enter business as trainee managers and future executives. Boys, on the other hand, tend to get day-release for craft and technical subjects at a junior level, and for professional qualifications when older.

FACTS

Out of school leavers up to 18 years:
2 out of 5 boys take up apprenticeships
1 in 14 girls take up apprenticeships

Department of Employment figures, 1970

Threequarters of these girls take apprenticeships in hairdressing – a traditionally female and badly paid occupation. A boy serving an apprenticeship may earn much less than a girl of the same age in another job, but in the long run his prospects are better than hers. Training facilities for young employees are being expanded, but little is being done to increase the number of girls using them. What is the reason for this bias, at a time when there is much talk of 'equal opportunity'? Employers are less willing to give girls an expensive training because they do not think they will get a good return on their money. They believe it will be 'wasted' because women will leave to get married and have children.

So, in this vicious circle, girls get the most monotonous and menial jobs, which tends to lower their ambition and makes them more willing to stop work anyway. It has been found that the higher the qualifications of a girl, the more likely she is to return quickly to skilled employment, thus not 'wasting' her skill. It is also true that having skills and expertise gives people confidence in all sorts of areas of their lives.

It is time employers became aware of the different career pattern that has emerged for women in the last decade. This pattern is: a five- to ten-year break from work for child-bearing, with a return to work before the age of thirty, and a possible thirty years' further employment. This makes it extremely worthwhile for the employer to re-train married women on their return to work, as well as training women in the first place.

WORK PATTERN OF TYPICAL MAN AND WOMAN

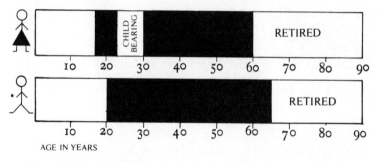

AGE IN YEARS

Often, firms offer different training to men and women when they start work. Men are invited to 'progress to managerial status', and to 'study for a professional qualification'. Their salaries will increase with the passing of exams. Women are invited to begin as clerical assistants or typists and 'to progress to become supervisors', but not managers or executives.

When they are in senior management and executive positions, women have been found to be as successful, if not more successful, then men. But lack of training means that they rarely reach these positions.

TEACHING A GIRL ABOUT HERTZ
IS TEACHING HER TO SAY YES

Before every new Hertz girl meets her public, she has to learn to always say Yes to a customer. It's easy when you work for Hertz because there's no limit to what Hertz has to offer. In fact, it takes us six weeks to fill her pretty head with all the facts and figures. We start off with the easy ones . . .

What we don't spell out in the book, we know a Hertz girl can handle naturally. We choose her because she's the kind of girl who enjoys solving all the little things that don't seem so little at the time.

73

Yes, I'll phone your wife to tell her you'll be late.

Yes, I'll find the briefcase you left in the car.

Yes, I'll sew the button on your coat.

The next time you want to rent a car, ask a Hertz girl.

You'll see how well she's learned her lessons.

Advertisement in The Times, 12 October 1972

Write off to any firms in the area you are likely to be employed in. Ask for their training schemes for school-leavers. Are there any differences between the sexes?
Are careers for women as important as careers for men?
How would you like to be trained as a Hertz girl?
Why don't they have Hertz boys?

3
THE
WORST WORK

Working in Woolie's

FACTS
1 out of 3 women workers are in industry
2 out of 5 service workers are women
from LEONORA LLOYD, *Women Workers in Britain*,
Socialist Women Publications

If you have few or no qualifications and do not get on-the-job training, you will most likely end up doing the worst work: the dirty, unpleasant, monotonous, badly paid worst work. For boys, it will be bad; but for girls, it will be THAT MUCH WORSE.

There are jobs in which all, or nearly all, the workers are women, and the pay is much lower than that of unskilled men. These are the 'female ghettoes'. They include the cleaners, the factory workers, the barmaids and waitresses, the shopworkers and the outworkers. Whether sitting at an assembly line, or serving the public, or sitting isolated in an office building, they are all in a similar position. And somewhere, there will be a man above them all.

Shopwork is one example of the type of service work that falls to women. There is worse – but for the majority of women the retail trade offers very little. There is no promotion and no responsibility; it is monotonous and tiring. In a large store, the work is soon likely to wear down any spark of enthusiasm or ambition that a girl has. Comments from three employees at a typical High Street shop, Woolworth's, show how this works in practice (our italics).

Tony, aged 23:
'I left school at fifteen. First I was a scientific instrument maker, then a sheet metal worker, trainee fruit and veg manager, and then this.

'They offer prospects here, I'm a trainee manager, I do the ordering, control the staff, do the displays. *I get a salary* which I'm happy with as I'm single; it wouldn't be enough if you were married.

'The training here is better than in most places, it holds good if you go to work in other stores. There are three others like me – all men. If I want something done, *I organize* the basic details and get one of the girls to carry it out.

'I like it here – there's always something new – *you never get bored.*'

Margaret, aged 16:
'This is my first job and I've been here a year – I used to work Saturdays, and I liked it, so I thought *I might as well* do full time. I left school because it got on my nerves. At the moment I earn £17 per week – that means I take home just over £15 after tax. I live at home – I couldn't afford not to.

'I expect I'll work here for a few years, and keep working full time after I get married. After the first few years I'll have kids. I don't really fancy the idea of going out to work after I'm married, so I'd look after the kids. Housework? It's not too bad.

'I'm *not really ambitious*, most of my friends are still at school, but I don't regret leaving early. I wouldn't call it a cushy job here, but the work is easy. The management are quite friendly and they don't push us. Sometimes *I get bored* if there's no stock. The only annoyance is the customers . . . It's no good a girl working here if she doesn't like shop work.'

Rose, aged 51 years:

'It's my fourth year here, I've always done jobs that *fit in with my family*. I've got three children, one boy of eleven is still at school. I work 9.30 to 1.30 five days, that way I can get him off to school before I go to work.

'You have to have a routine – I get up at about six and do the washing and ironing early in the morning.

'I get £11 for a twenty-hour week . . . I don't earn enough to pay tax. My reasons for working . . . first *for the money*, and also interest. *A few hours' break* from the home, mixing with people, the people are nice here.

'I'm quite satisfied with the money, but it's not good if you are young – they can go for better work. Some of them leave for office work – it's more money and they don't like working on Saturdays. They can't get women to do full-time – most of us are part-timers – well, if you've got a family you've got to *cater for them*.'

There were no men AT ALL serving at the counters, or working part-time. Why do you think this is? There were no women trainee managers – only supervisors dealing with staff. There was an absolute division here between the better jobs, for men, and the drudgery, for the women. What possible grounds can there be for women not managing a store, and men not serving at counters? What could a store like Woolworth's do to change this situation?

The information for new recruits offers different prospects for men and for women. If a trainee is the right type of man he can manage a store after five years and earn up to £6,000. If an assistant proves capable, she will be put in charge of a department to help the manager, or she can become a staff supervisor, instructor or cashier. While a man is receiving a training that will lead him into a good position, here or in any other job, women are being taught such 'skills' as how to wrap goods and how to serve the customer.

Of course, there is one very valuable bonus for the women.

'If a full-time female employee marries after three years she receives an *ex gratia* wedding present.' The compensation for being a woman?

In what kinds of stores and departments do you find women as managers? Where do you find male assistants?

Do you really think that women do the worst work in our society? For example, some people would argue that men do the really worst jobs, such as mining. What do you think the worst jobs are?

Would it be a good idea to have more people sharing the worst jobs on a part-time basis?

Why do people do part-time work? Do you think there are enough opportunities for men to work part-time? Would many of them want to?

Immigrant women – the worst of the worst work

Immigrant women on the job market are in a worse position than white women. They are a pool of unskilled labour, often doing work that is seasonal or on shifts, the worst paid and the least secure, in the worst conditions.

FACTS

1 in every 10 West Indian women works in textiles

1 in every 5 West Indian women works in the service industries

---

Usually they are found in the dirtiest and lowest-grade jobs – cleaning, washing up and working in laundries and dry cleaners, where they are not actually seen by the public.

Not only is the work bad but there are other problems, such as language difficulties, especially for Asian women, and the consequent lack of communication with other workers. This can make it very hard for them to alter their conditions.

Many West Indian women are the only providers for their children. So shift work and low pay are doubly hard on them.

A high proportion of immigrant women are registered unemployed. One survey in an industrial town showed that two out of every five unemployed women were immigrant. So they are the first to suffer from cutbacks, and are therefore the most vulnerable workers.

Here are some facts to illustrate the position of immigrant women in relation to the labour market in this country. They provide the cheapest form of labour, and are often untrained for better-paid jobs, or unable to work the hours these jobs demand. They come at the bottom of the ladder in low-paid jobs.

Unskilled man	*Unskilled white woman*	*Unskilled immigrant woman*
CHEAP	CHEAPER	CHEAPEST

We could substitute the word WEAK here, because this is what the work for immigrant women shows about the position of women in our society. It is those who are in a weak position to fight for themselves who get the worst deal of all.

4
TRADITIONALLY
FEMALE OCCUPATIONS

Nursing, or patients are a virtue

Girls with any ambition may well find themselves in one of the traditionally female jobs which have for a long time been considered 'suitable' and 'respectable' for them to do. One such job is nursing. Nowadays, men do go into nursing, of course, but in very small numbers. Ever wondered why?

FACTS

95% of nurses are women, 5% are men.
80% of doctors are men, 20% are women.

from LEONORA LLOYD, *Women Workers in Britain*,
Socialist Women Publications

Clearly the pay that nurses get, after three years' training to be a State Registered Nurse, or two years to be a State Enrolled Nurse, is a big drawback, to say the least. 'It is not a man's wage' is the comment you will hear many people make on this state of affairs.

Nurses are always being told what wonderful people they are, what a vital job they are doing. This image pressurizes them into accepting their low wages as a fact of life. Their reward is being appreciated.

Do you always think of nurses as being women?
Are there any reasons why men aren't suited to be nurses?
What jobs do men do in hospitals – apart from being doctors?

'My secretary is a lovable slave' (U.S. Senator)

Two out of every five girls who leave school under the age of eighteen go into office work. It's hard to imagine that when typewriters and telephones were first invented men thought they were far too complicated for women ever to operate. But with the introduction of more machines into offices, a clear division has developed between the 'organizational and managerial' side for men, and the 'mechanical' work of typing and shorthand for women. If you get on really well, you may become a 'secretary', or even a 'personal assistant,' but you will always, or almost always, have a man boss; you will be working 'for' someone else, performing the more menial tasks for him. A typist can never cross over that boundary line into the world where men make the decisions and run the show. She may know everything there is to know about her job and the firm she works for. But when her boss retires, there's rarely any question of the secretary taking his place.

Here is an account of office work by a typist of the top grade (our italics):

Joyce, aged 21 years:
'I've no idea why I went in for office work . . . it just came about . . . I never planned a career really.

'I did a full-time course at college, typing, shorthand and some O levels. They found me my first job. There I was *general dogsbody*: I had to go to the post office because I was the youngest, then to the shop for their pasties and cakes – I didn't like that. I had to *make hundreds of cups of coffee* in case there were visitors, and there were never enough cups. I got £8 a week for that. I stayed nine months, but when I asked for a rise they refused, so I decided to look somewhere else.

'Then I went temping. That's nice – they don't expect you to do much, they don't stick a load of responsibility on you. I want to find a place I like before I can be bothered with them. Once I gave up working for nine months – it just didn't seem

worth working for the money I was getting – £12 a week, and that was for a top grade shorthand-typist at the age of twenty. If I went to a better paid job it would have cost me in fares. They always promised to pay you travel allowance, but they never did.

'Then I came to London, where the money's much better. I get £120 a month, and I could get a lot more if I went temping – £45 a week – but I'd rather have a job that I like. I like it where I am now because the people are nice, and also I get six weeks' paid holiday as it is at the university. My boss is *very considerate* – he asks me if I want to do something, and if I say I don't he won't ask me again. Also we all just have a good chat – sometimes we are very busy, but other days I hardly do anything at all.

'Typing – it's not really interesting work. I'm mostly typing chemistry reports that I don't understand. I'd like to be doing other things apart from typing. I'd also like to change the pay – to be paid by ability instead of age.

'In other places I've got annoyed when the men would come in and expect you to *drop everything* just to make them coffee. In some places it's just the way they look at you. At one firm you had to go upstairs to some offices and they would stand at the bottom to look up your skirt. When they are talking they make remarks to try to embarrass you. Once when I was 17 a married man of 40 kept asking me out. I used to tell him not to be disgusting. I think they just show themselves up when they are together. In firms where they have a lot of work, though, they are too busy to bother about that sort of thing.

'If you were a boy you wouldn't have old men making advances at you. Also they wouldn't put upon you to do these *little errands* – they'd expect boys to be cheekier. If I'd have turned round and refused I'd have got the sack.'

At the higher end of the scale, the secretary is usually more closely attached to her one boss. She has to protect him from intruders, to appear as an ornament and status symbol in his office. She tends not to have a status and function of her own – she is X's secretary. Rather like a mother and housewife, she is never really noticed or appreciated until she is no longer there. She performs the 'invisible' tasks that make things run smoothly and which most men prefer not to notice.

Compare the 'male' interpretation of the word 'secretary' – the company secretary, who is an administrative worker. Only two per cent of the Institute of Chartered Secretaries are women. One careers manual explains this phenomenon for us:

> 'The highly specialised nature of a company secretary's work makes continuity of service within a company an extremely important consideration, and this could clash with a woman's domestic responsibilities.'
>
> from *A Careers Guide for School Leavers*

The apathy expressed by typists in the pool, their lack of interest in their jobs and the tendency to seek satisfaction outside of work all show how mechanical this job is. Many turn to 'temping' – it offers a change of scene and better pay, and even less responsibility. It is always someone else's ideas that have to be typed out; nothing is ever produced by the typist herself. It is very hard for them to improve their conditions because they can be coaxed, flattered, charmed, if not victimized, by their bosses.

Is there any reason why men shouldn't be typists?
Do women really prefer to work for men?

Teaching – join the professionals

Is there a job that offers complete equality for men and women including equal pay?
What about teaching?

But don't look too closely, or you might be disappointed.

FACTS
1. **There are three times as many women as men in primary teaching.**
2. **The average salary for all women in primary schools is about £400 lower than that of men.**
3. **There are two-thirds as many women as men in secondary schools.**
4. **The average salary for all women in secondary schools is about £300 lower than that of men.**

from *Statistics in Education*, D.E.S., 1972

The lowest paid teachers are those in infant and primary schools, the highest paid are in colleges and universities. Women make up the majority of teachers of the young. So the younger the child, the more likely it is to be taught by a woman. And the less money she is likely to be paid for doing it!

The trend for men to get higher pay is in fact INCREASING. Pay rises between 1960 and 1970 were about £100 more for men primary teachers than women. The reason for this is that it is mostly men who get the higher paid senior posts. What's more, the effect of equal pay in teaching has been to *reduce* the numbers of headships given to women. Since it is no longer cheaper to appoint a woman, authorities have shown that they *prefer* to appoint a man.

	1961	1971
Men as heads	15,000	17,500 (approx.)
Women as heads	14,000	11,000 (approx.)

from *Statistics in Education*, D.E.S., 1972

So, instead of equal numbers of men and women heads, there are now far more men than women. This includes primary schools, where the teachers are mostly women. One-third of men in primary schools who are non-graduate teachers become headmasters. Only one in twelve non-graduate women do the same. Two out of three women are still on Scale I in primary schools, but only one in four men are.

What are the reasons for women being so far behind in the race for promotion? Partly it is prejudice on the part of those making appointments. Women often complain that they are asked questions at interviews like: 'Are you planning to get married, have a baby?' How many men are asked such questions? Since the reorganization of secondary schools into comprehensives, the usual practice is to make the headmaster of the boys' school the head, and the headmistress of the girls' school the deputy head.

However, many women in their middle or late twenties do have children, and because in teaching promotion is given for continuous service it is they who lose out. They suffer because of what is a biological fact: they don't get the best jobs because it is they who have the children. And they suffer because of a social fact: they remain responsible for them.

Since men cannot have children, a change in attitude to a woman's career is obviously needed. If maternity leave were made longer than it is at present, it would be possible for the many women who want to, to take advantage of it instead of having to resign. If training were made available for married women who return to work in their early thirties, then they would be able to qualify for better jobs instead of finding that their knowledge of the job is out of date.

The higher ranks of education are even more dominated by men:

	Men	Women
Chief education officers	162	2
Deputy chief officers	132	2
Divisional chief officers	90	2
Assistant education officers	282	18
Assistant members	46	2
	712	26

from EILEEN BYRNE, *Education, Training and Equal Opportunity*

There are no women out of 44 university vice-chancellors, 44 registrars and 42 heads of university departments of education. Only five per cent of the heads of mixed comprehensive schools, and three per cent of the heads of colleges of further education are women. At the same time. there has recently been a campaign to get married women back to teaching. So, it seems, 'a woman teacher's place is in the classroom'. With its convenient hours, long holidays and opportunities for part-time work, classroom teaching is 'woman's work'; but when it comes to the better paid administrative work and greater responsibility . . . then men take over.

At which stage of education is the teacher more important – primary or secondary, nursery school or college?
Which teachers should be the most highly rewarded?

5
WOMEN IN
A MAN'S WORLD

'Exceptional creatures'

There are some women who are successful in fields of work that are dominated by men. They range from politicians, executives and scientists with a high level of training to decorators, plumbers and drivers with manual skills and strength. Whatever the job, these women have some experiences in common: they have to PROVE themselves equal to men; they are considered the 'exception', somehow 'different' from ordinary women; and whether in the canteen of the Houses of Parliament or in a transport café, they are very likely to come up against male attitudes and prejudice.

They are probably better off than women who are doing 'women's work', but they are under a form of pressure because they are in a minority, and they have to be strong-minded to succeed. There are so few of them that they cannot look to each other for support; they are effectively isolated. Obviously, if some women can do these jobs, then many more could too; but social influences at the moment do not lead most women in this direction, and it requires a particular ambition to break away. Also, 'men's work' is often more difficult to combine with the 'second' job of running the family, since this is a responsibility men rarely take. Therefore women have a second problem, and it seems that an understanding husband or a single life are essential to do these exceptional jobs.

A female Member of Parliament has this to say (our italics):

'The main problem is having to always do a second job – making sure your husband has clean shirts, seeing that the cleaning is done. Even if someone does it for you, *you have the responsibility*. You can never delegate responsibility unless you are very wealthy indeed. You are always in charge of the housekeeping money.

'It is essential in a family situation to have a *husband who supports you* one hundred per cent. You would have to be either single or divorced, or have their full co-operation to be in public life . . . otherwise you would be a very unhappy woman.

'The reform of the House, limiting evening hours, would allow more women to sit but this will never seriously be considered by the men; they would have to go home and maybe read a bed-time story. It's like a middle-aged boys' public school here; they have the whips for their prefects, there are the school bullies and the nice boys. *Parliament is a male institution* . . . the Speaker, officers and clerks are all men. Women always have to carry the family; just as in a working-class home the man goes to the pub with his mates, so here they can stay in the House with their mates . . . it's the same thing. There are so few women in public life that it is comparatively easy to get in, and once you have made it, it's very fair. One of the problems of women is that they limit themselves too much, far too much. You have to be very determined, and able to accept being batted down, and to be friendly afterwards.

'There is a lot of chauvinism. When I made my second speech it was on the subject of North Sea oil. The men teased me because *it wasn't a woman's subject* – they were rather patronizing. On my first day in the House I was waiting in the canteen when a man I've known for a long time said, "I'm glad you've got here, and now you're here I hope you'll do something about the dreadful food!" I replied, "You do something about the food – I'm more interested in the Chancellor of the Exchequer!" He looked open-mouthed and realized his mistake.

'You have to be careful that you are not put on to "women's subjects". When I was on the Prices Committee they wanted me to put the *housewives' point of view*. I refused – I wanted to represent the shopper – male or female. It's also hard to get away from the idea of the Statutory Woman – they feel that if they put a woman on each committee it is a sop to the fact that 51 per cent of voters are women. Then when I'm on a committee *I'm not expected to contribute* . . . yet I don't do so just because I'm a woman, but only when I want to say something.

'In public life we suffer from the Maverick Woman – the middle-class committee woman who *makes eyes at the men*. She is the biggest nuisance when you want to get things done. They do consider you "unusual" if you are in public life . . . that is the tragedy . . . you become the "pet", the "*exceptional creature*", and this affects you if you are not very careful. I'd like a situation in which women are valued for the contribution they make.

'Women will take up a case and fight it, if it has been put to them and they feel it is genuine. Men have been trained from an early age to hide their feelings and to be extra careful in dealing with the public. I've noticed that in general women M.P.s get bigger post-bags than the men. They write the sort of letters that don't finish the case – one I know of has gone on for seven years, while men will be more inclined to deal with an issue with one reply.

'Things are changing. But in politics we have stood still since the Suffragettes. I would like to make a Private Member's Bill to get equal numbers of men and women on all public bodies by law – this is a necessary step towards equal participation by women. Then women officers would make a real effort to get more women into public life, and girls would be educated for it at school.'

Find out how many women M.P.s there are in Parliament at the moment.
Why do you think men tend to be more interested in politics than women?

Women in the Services – 'adding the feminine touch'

As you would expect, women who join the Services do not find themselves in a position of greater equality than anywhere else. Take the Navy: the women's section, the W.R.N.S., are able to work with sailors – but not doing the same things, for the Wrens are not encouraged to compete with men. They may do some dirty jobs, but they are encouraged to look as smart and attractive as possible, both in uniform and out of it.

As for the work Wrens are actually involved in, the main point is that they do not go to sea, but serve on shore. So what would be the chief attraction for a man joining the Navy – going to sea – is not the one for a woman, whose job it is to serve the Naval officers, who are men.

It's a similar story in the Army. The aim and object of the Women's Royal Army Corps is to 'free men for their fighting role by taking over any duty which a woman can effectively perform'. So women free men to fight – possibly if they were allowed to do any more they might be in a position to question the whole point of fighting at all! So if you thought that Army life for women was only for those hard enough and tough enough to cope, you will be surprised to learn that it is in fact a very feminine occupation. As the recruiting leaflet says: 'It all adds up to an extremely busy and varied life, including paper work, people, technical problems and adding the feminine touch!' In complete contrast, every aspect of extreme masculinity is stressed for the males – the work is described as exciting, demanding, challenging; it is action-packed, needs skill and toughness, and is designed to make 'men' of its raw recruits.

Get hold of recruiting literature for the Army, Navy and Air Force. Compare the way men and women are presented. For example, you may notice that in the material aimed at men, no women are involved, but when it is aimed at women, the stress is always on men.

By tradition the Services, law, banking, the Church were ideal careers for men. Nowadays women play a part in them: but find out for yourself exactly what it is they have been allowed to do. Should there be women priests?

Should women who join the Army be allowed to fight alongside the men?

6
WOMEN ON SALE:
THE SEXPLOITATION JOBS

There is another category of jobs that is almost exclusively the domain of women and which is unconnected with home or children. These are the 'sexploitation' jobs, which at least offer good money.

These jobs include fashion and photographic modelling – which are not on the surface exploitative of women – through to prostitution, the most degrading of all to women. In between these two extremes are the hired escorts, the hostesses, the bunny girls and pets and strip-tease dancers.

But why should women earning a living in these ways be regarded as exploited? What's wrong with being a topless go-go dancer or a bunny girl, if that's what people want to do? One answer to that could well be: if there's nothing wrong with it, why aren't men doing it?

Women in these sexploitation jobs are not treated as people, as individuals, but as saleable bodies, merchandise. The essence of sexploitation jobs is that what is 'sold' is not one's time or labour or skill, but oneself, in the very real sense of one's body.

It is this selling of a part of oneself, with the emphasis on the sexual parts, that makes these jobs degrading and exploitative of women. This is not only degrading for the women who do them, but ultimately for all women and also for the men who feel the need for their services. But then, what real choice do women who do these jobs have? If the alternative is the mind-deadening routine of the typing pool or the assembly line, with their lack of real opportunity, it is easy enough to look for what appear to be easier ways of making a living at jobs such as these, where the money is better.

Pets and Bunnies, or the alternative world of waitressing

Being a Playboy Bunny or a Penthouse Pet is basically waitressing work with the doubtful privilege of having to look sexy into the bargain. This effect is heightened by the highly stylized fantasy costumes that have to be worn. 'A girl doesn't have to be all that well-built to work as a bunny – *we can always stuff tissue paper in the cups* to pad her out a bit', we were told, when we asked what kind of girls they looked for. 'The bunnies wear ears to keep their hair out of their eyes and off the face – it's a *catering regulation*', while the pet costumes at another club are '*daring and provocative*. What the pets wear is the nearest thing to a French maid's costume that could be designed. They are *very saucy* – especially while waiting on tables.' According to the girls who work at the clubs, the main attraction is the 'glamour', the chance to earn good money, the chance to meet well-known people, and the chance to meet rich men, one of whom they might possibly marry.

The turn-over at these places is very high, with few girls lasting very long. Very few qualifications are needed: youth, good looks, a good figure and 'a nice smile's very important'.

Why are there no clubs with Bunny Boys?

Prostitution – large chest for sale

While the actual practice is allowed, the law operates against prostitutes in various ways. A woman can be arrested and charged for soliciting, that is for trying to attract clients on the street. She is permitted to carry on her occupation if it is kept behind locked doors and away from the public eye. She can advertise in metaphors – 'French classes available' – but plain language is regarded as offensive. If a woman tries to solicit it is called 'harassment', but if a man tries to do the same it is called 'flattery', and any woman would be ridiculed who tried to bring him to Court.

It is argued that prostitutes are independent, both financially and personally. But high pay doesn't make them the equal of their clients. The .very fact that the only way these women have found to earn a decent income is by making themselves totally physically dependent on the sexual demands of men means that they are not free. The fact that men ridicule them and treat them as inferior to other women means that prostitutes are paying the price of public scorn for their earnings. Few men have to do this.

It is a job that affects the prostitute's whole life and her relationships with all men – and in a damaging way.

The prostitute has to be polite and agree with her client's views, because he has paid not only for sex but also for her company, and this woman's company is supposed to be AGREE-ABLE. This is the worst part of the job – that she has to surrender the right to be herself.

Would prostitution be necessary in a society where men and women were equal?

'It's spoiled my relationships with men. It's very hard to be common property like that and to find a man who will put up with it. The social stigma attached to prostitution is a very powerful thing. It makes a kind of total state out of prostitution so that the whore is always a whore. It is as if you did it once – you become it. That makes it very easy for people to get locked into it.'

from KATE MILLET, *The Prostitution Papers*, Paladin

It has been argued that there are degrees of prostitution. Would you say that a girl who goes out with a man she dislikes for the expensive meals, etc., is in a small way acting like a prostitute?

7
ONLY A HOUSEWIFE

The nature of housework

How often have you heard:
A woman's place is in the home
Housewives are such boring people
All women do is gossip all day
A woman's work is never done
All you do is cook and clean and sit around all day

There are two inescapable facts about full-time housework:

(1) *The isolation.* Housewives are alone all day to work by themselves, usually only with very young children for company, and so their contact with the outside world is limited. They meet each other while shopping, or drop round to each others' houses for coffee.

(2) *The demoralizing routine.* It is argued that the housewife doesn't have the boss breathing over her shoulder every five minutes, she can plan her own routine, have a cigarette whenever she likes, or take a break. Surely that is preferable to a really boring, routine job in a factory? But what people who don't do housework do not realize is that the work itself is more relentless than any boss – simply because it is never finished, while young children must be looked after almost around the clock.

In fact a lot of young women actually look forward to the day they can give up the boring, badly paid jobs they work at for what they imagine to be the 'freedom' of staying at home while

their husbands go out to earn the money. The majority of such women soon find, however, that it is not the easy option they imagined. They have lost the financial independence they once had as well as the social contact that comes with having a paid job. Many women doing part-time work, even if very badly paid, are grateful for the chance 'just to get out of the house for a break' or 'just for the company'. Many women with no work besides housework become increasingly dissatisfied and depressed with their role in life. Some women, it is true, do find it satisfying, but they are few in number; for many, full-time housework can be demoralizing work.

FACT

A great number of full-time housewives seek treatment from their G.P.s for such ailments as depression, tiredness, fatigue, 'nervous complaints' . . . They are prescribed tranquillizers, pep-pills, anti-depressants, sleeping pills. Why?

One of the most demoralizing aspects of housework is the never-ending routine of most of it – it is never finished. No sooner is the floor swept than it needs doing again, or a meal is cooked and a few hours later another one has to be prepared and the dishes washed. So the housewife rarely has the satisfaction of finishing anything, or of feeling that after a certain time the job is over and done with.

HOUSEWORK EXPANDS TO FILL IN THE TIME AVAILABLE TO DO IT

'. . . many frantically busy full-time housewives were amazed to find that they could polish off in one hour the housework that used to take them six – or was still undone at dinnertime – as soon as they started studying, or working, or had some interest outside the home.'

from BETTY FRIEDAN, *The Feminine Mystique*, Penguin

In other words, if you have a whole day in which to do the household chores, then those chores will take you the whole day.

 ## 'I don't work, I'm only a housewife'

> **Think how often you have heard these expressions:**
> **She's staying home now that she's got married.**
> **She's not at work this week.**
> **Her husband doesn't like her working.**
> **I don't do anything – I'm only a housewife.**
> **I'm not going to work once I'm married.**

All these expressions convey the same idea: that housework and bringing up children are not really work. But why is this? Anyone who actually does housework or cleaning for someone else for a living will tell you that housework *is* work, just as much as working in a shop or office is work.

The only difference is that housework *as such* is not regarded as work since it is not paid for. 'Real' work is measured by cash, 'real' work is paid for; housework on the other hand is not paid for, it is merely done. Nothing is actually produced that can be sold or which can make a profit. The housewife only produces and looks after the future workers of society.

Housework is either work or it isn't.
If it is work, then it is either useful or it isn't.
All work useful to society is paid for.
Housework is not paid for.
Therefore it is not useful to society.

What do you think?

Doing two jobs

Among the reasons women give for choosing to go out to work, the following stand out:

(1) purely financial – 'We need the money.'

(2) emotional satisfaction – 'I'd go mad staying in the house all day.'

(3) intellectual reasons – 'I was trained to do this job, so I would be wasted not doing it.'

For many women, their circumstances are such that they have to work. For some the choice between staying at home or going out to work is never actually made; it is automatically assumed that they will work for a living and it does not occur to them to stay at home unless they are compelled to do so.

These figures show the number of mothers with school-age children who work outside the home:

21% of all mothers with children 0 to 4 years old work.
46% of mothers with children 5 to 10 years old work.
from *Survey of Women's Employment*, a government social survey, 1968, and the 1971 Census

Would the percentage be higher if there were more nursery facilities or if the fathers took an equal share of work in the home?

On these women are likely to fall two additional burdens:

(1) the problem of making arrangements for the care of their children, which is more difficult the younger they are;

(2) the responsibility of seeing that the necessary minimum of cooking, cleaning and shopping is done.

Remember that in most families these two items are regarded as being the primary concern of the wife, not of the husband (no visitor is going to think it's the man's fault if the house is a mess). No one is likely to suggest to potential fathers that they find jobs where the hours are flexible enough to fit in with bringing up a family. Nor is it a general thing for fathers to have time off work (paternity leave), or for them to campaign for creches and day nurseries at their factories and places of work. It seems to be unfair to both sexes that one sex should have the total responsibility for the care and upbringing of children, while the burden of being 'breadwinner' and sole financial supporter should fall on the other. How many men might prefer to be given the chance to stay at home and look after the house and children, while their wives worked?

So, are there any alternatives to the situation where women are either:

(1) full-time housewives;

(2) doing two jobs, one full-time and the other running the home?

Some possible alternatives could be:

(a) more part-time work for men, so that husband and wife could share the upbringing of children and earning a living;

(b) not only maternity leave for women but paternity leave for men, so that they can play a fuller part in the upbringing of their own children, allowing men as well as women time off from work for family responsibilities;

(c) more day care centres and crèches so that children can be looked after in an organized group, rather than just being 'minded';

(d) shared housework so that this is no longer mainly the woman's job.

It would be good at least to have the choice, so that men are not *automatically* assumed to have to go out and earn a living, and women are not *automatically* considered to be naturally better suited to home-making and child-rearing.

Story
by Shirley Moreno

She was a good woman – pretty, happy, and very loving. She enjoyed her work – getting up early, bustling about with the kids, talking about school, games and Christmas. Christmas was a month away and the children were very excited. Anyhow, once the kids were off to school she started her work proper. She dusted, cleaned, washed and mended.

The best part of the day for her was cooking the evening meal. She loved the anticipation of the family coming home to her warm, snug kitchen and all of them together eating her meal that she had made for them. She liked to make it as much a part of her as she could. She liked to feel it was her daily creation for their flesh to grow on – that she herself had made their flesh by making their food.

Today, however, she was very worried. All the time she was doing the hoovering and listening to Jimmy Young she worried. By the time she reached her mid-day snack she was still worrying. And even in the afternoon while she was polishing the windows (a job she usually saved for 'difficult days' because she enjoyed it so much), she still carried on thinking about her problem – what to cook tonight.

She had been all through Marguerite Patten's *Meat Cookery* twice and *The Encyclopedia of Spanish Cookery* three times. Life was so hard. He didn't like garlic or peppers. Jo did not care for onions, cheese or cream, and Jane hated greens, cauliflower and fish. They weren't eating as well as they used to. Even their favourite meals were no longer greeted with the usual shouts of glee. And she was sure Jo had lost weight . . . it was all so worrying . . . what could she do?

As she listened to Terry Wogan's happy chatter she nibbled fretfully on a Golden Delicious, then a Snib's Peanut Cracker, and was half-way through a Ginger Crunch before she realized what she was doing. Remembering her calorie-controlled diet, she put the remains of the biscuit in the cat's plate and walked into the kitchen.

She flicked through her cookery books, disconcerted. Suddenly she saw it. Laminated brains in milk sauce. The perfect
answer! But where would they sell brains? She had never seen
them in the butcher's. Then she realized – would she dare?
What a perfect idea, why had she not thought of it before?

She went into the bathroom and looked around – a nail file,
perfect! She leaned over the hand basin, so as not to stain the
new poly-saturated nyrostyrane tiles on the bathroom floor
and stared into her husband's shaving mirror. She made a hole
with the nail file just above her right ear. It would have been
better at the back but it was very difficult to see, so she settled
for just above the ear. She made the hole just large enough for
her hand. At first she could not find them, but after some grop-
ing about she got them at last – down by her nasal passage. They
were small but very loosely attached so they came out easily.
She put them for the time being in the sink and patched the
hole in her head with some Elastoplasts. When she had combed
her hair over and lacquered it you could hardly tell.

That evening the family arrived home to a delicious smell.
'Oh, Mum, Mum, what a wonderful smell; we're starving!'
They shed their clothes in the hall, put chocolate fingers on the
window, tripped over the coffee table upsetting the Christmas-
flowering geraniums, and arrived in the kitchen.

They were all silent as she took the steaming dish from the
oven. For one awful moment she thought they might guess.
They would never eat it if they knew where she had got it
from; but they didn't notice how like her it looked. She served
them a tiny portion each. They looked surprised. 'That all?'
they said. Next day she was sure Jane was a little tiny bit taller,
and Jo's hair was so shiny . . .

In the morning she felt a little faint and had to rest during
'Soft Spot for Mums', but by afternoon tea she was fine – she
had decided to try kidney that night. It was more difficult this
time, she wasn't quite sure where they were, but third time she
got them. The Elastoplasts didn't stick quite so well, so she put

on her tightest roll-on. The meal was devoured by all three of them in silence. She was so pleased . . . Next day they had rump steak, then spare rib, then liver.

The day they had the liver there was nearly a catastrophe. The roll-on seemed to have stretched because it wasn't as tight as it used to be. Anyway it must have leaked because when he came home through the front door there was a small pool of blood just by the tufted coconut-hair mat (53p from Woolworth's in the sale). He was pretty mad at coming home to such a mess and it took her a long time to calm him down. By the time he had had his braised liver he was in fine spirits, and agreed to forgive her, as long as it never happened again.

Then they had marrow soup, belly meat, a good cut of shoulder, some stewed lung and then half a roast head. She was amazed they did not notice but as long as she didn't make a mess they didn't seem to see. She was wonderfully pleased that they were so healthy; not a cold among them and Jane had grown a whole half inch. Even he seemed fuller somehow, the creases in his cheeks were gone and he had a puffy, smooth look like an American film star.

Her only worry now was that there seemed to be much more housework than there used to be and she found it difficult to get round. She had noticed some dust the other day on top of the Bush full-colour transistor television (four channels), and realized that she had forgotten to dust that day. She could not believe it. It had never happened before.

Then they had neck, a cut of shin and some sausages made with blood and offal. The family was looking wonderful. They were all taller and fatter.

Christmas grew nearer. She was planning a real treat for Christmas, but it was a lot of work. Never had it been so hard for her to get through her work and prepare for Christmas. What was more, the family had started to notice. He was very worried about it. His socks were crumpled and twice that week he could not find a clean hanky. She could sense his anger and contempt for her lack of order but somehow she felt incapable of changing. Whatever she did, things went wrong. Even if she carried on work in the evening he would moan at the noise and inconvenience for him, and go out, slamming the door. The children sensed the change in her too, and took advantage of it by playing up terribly.

She kept on working doggedly towards the high spot of her year, Christmas, and especially the dinner. Working against her always was a growing feeling of tiredness and giddiness – she could not explain, maybe she was just tired. She allowed herself the luxury of a morning in bed a few days before Christmas, but when she got up she felt no better, even perhaps a bit wobbly on her knees. She took three aspirins and a drink of Lucozade and got on with the mincemeat and forcemeats.

Christmas Day dawned bright and clear. Strong loud voices reverberated through the house, proclaiming their youth and joy; presents, paper and string everywhere. Getting up slow and cold, Sellotape on my foot. What a long way to the bathroom. Phlegm in my throat, blood on my leg. Quick, bolt the door, good. First spit, what choking in my throat. Next, my leg. It's dribbled down to my foot. Where is the Tampax? Here. Rip – sod, the thread always breaks. In, go on, up. Now roll-on – (sigh) – long-line, cross-your-heart bra. Elastic stockings. I feel better now, as if I were properly together now I have my clothes on.

She went to the bathroom and bolted the door. She must have dressed in there. She took long enough and was fully clothed when she came out.

'Hello.'

'Hello.'

Downstairs – breakfast – wash up – clean table – brush floor – empty rubbish bin – adjust central heating.

Wonderful, I am alone at last. It's in the fridge. I left it there last night. It must be completely frozen now – looks so dark and red and completely hard.

    take one heart

    soak it

salt it
shake it
braise it -
add finely chopped nut
graized word
$\frac{1}{2}$ baked book
2 pinches love and lump it
1 bay leaf
Bash the heart well, stuff it and rape it, roll it well around, mix it with essence of hate and sprinkle liberally with loneliness and isolation.

She served the heart. They ate it. She died that afternoon, after washing up, so they had to have a cold tea.

from *Women's Liberation Review*, Vol. 1,
October 1972 (Women's Liberation Collective)

Attitudes to housework: 'I don't mind sharing the housework', or man about the house: guide to avoiding housework

(1) Yes, I'll give you a hand but I've got something important to do right now.

(Meaning he'd rather be reading the newspaper.)

(2) Yes, I'll give you a hand – but let's both do the things we're best at.

(Meaning he'd rather be changing a light bulb while she washes dishes.)

(3) Yes, I'll give you a hand but you'll have to show me how to do it.

(Meaning I've never cleaned the oven – and I don't intend to start now.)

(4) Yes, I'll give you a hand – but I'm going to do it my way.

(Meaning if I do it my way the dishes get done once a week, not after every meal.)

(5) Yes, I'll give you a hand – but if you want it done better than

OH CLUMSY ME! PERHAPS I'D BETTER LEAVE YOU TO IT.

YOU START DEAR, I'LL BE THERE IN A MOMENT.

LIKE THIS DEAR, ARE YOU GETTING THE IDEA NOW?...

SHE'LL NEVER THINK OF LOOKING UNDER HERE

YOU CAN'T SERIOUSLY EXPECT ME TO DESERT FULHAM WHEN THEY'RE 3-1 DOWN – FOR YOUR... DISHES

MY HANDS ARE NOT GOING INSIDE THAT!

this you'll have to do it yourself.

(Meaning I'll make such a mess of it that it'll be quicker if she does it herself.)

(6) Yes, I'll give you a hand – but if you think I'm going to do *that*, forget it.

(Meaning you won't catch me cleaning the lavatory.)

(7) Yes, I'll give you a hand – but I'm not that fussy about how the place looks, and who's going to notice this anyway?

(Meaning I'll annoy you by sweeping under the carpet.)

(8) Yes, I'll give you a hand – but I don't know where things are supposed to go.

(Meaning I might have lived here as long as she has, but it's her job to look after me.)

Which of the following list of household jobs do you think are best done or should be done by women, which by men, and which equally by both?

fixing a fuse	sewing on the machine
mending a plug	vacuuming the carpets
fitting shelves	cleaning the windows
moving furniture	changing nappies
reading bedtime stories	tidying up
bathing the baby	building an extension
making the breakfast	unblocking the drains
emptying the bins	stripping the paintwork
peeling potatoes	wallpapering
shopping for food	mending clothes
choosing the curtains	

Are there any areas that you personally would label as being exclusively women's work?

The housewife's story (page 101): although the story is a surrealistic one, what point is its author trying to convey? What is your reaction?

Think about the way in which you were brought up. Who did what around the house? What jobs did the male members of your family do in the house? Why?

Talk to a housewife you know and ask her what she thinks about the work she does, what satisfaction she gets out of it. Did she have to give up any ideals or ambitions when she got married in order to run a home and bring up children?

What are the possible alternatives to the isolation of individual housewives? Would such things as communal laundries, kitchens and child-care groups help? Do women want them?

Would you bring up your children to be responsible for cleaning up after themselves and to help with the housework – or do you think it is the mother's job to do it for them?

Find out the current rates of pay per hour for cleaning private houses, and for babysitting. Compare them with the hourly rate for any unskilled manual work. If there is a discrepancy, how do you account for it?

What do you think of the idea of getting wages for housework?

AND THE LAST WORD ON THE SUBJECT:

ON A TIRED HOUSEWIFE

Here lies a poor woman who was always tired,
She lived in a house where help wasn't hired.
Her last words on earth were: Dear friends, I am going
To where there's no cooking or washing, or sewing.
For everything there is exact to my wishes,
For where they don't eat there's no washing of dishes.
I'll be where loud anthems will always be ringing
But having no voice I'll be quit of the singing.
Don't mourn for me now, don't mourn for me never,
I am going to do nothing for ever and ever.

Anon., reprinted by courtesy of Shrew

8
WOMEN AND
TRADE UNIONS

'Trade unionists, their wives and families'

---

3 out of every 5 women work in jobs done only by women.
For every £1 earned by men in this country, women earn
50p.
In 1973, the average weekly wage for all men was £40.9.
In 1973, the average weekly wage for all women was £22.6.

from LEONORA LLOYD, *Women Workers in Britain*,
Socialist Women Publications

Trade unions are, by and large, male institutions. Unionists
even talk at times as if all of their members were men, perhaps
addressing audiences as 'brothers'. But one in four trade
unionists are women, and they are joining unions at twice the
rate of men.

Why is it, then, that the unionists we see on television making
bargains with the government are all men?

Why do we usually hear in the news of women either 'backing'
their husbands in a strike or begging them to return to work?

The way in which unions are organized makes it difficult for
women to attend meetings, because they are more tied to the
home than men, and meetings are often held at inconvenient
times for women with children. When they do attend, they may
have a harder time being listened to. So it is not surprising to
find so few women trade union officials.

Women also often lack the confidence – a confidence that most men have – to speak in public. Nor are they encouraged to organize and run things, as men are.

The night cleaners – 'working for luxuries'?

> 'In all my years in the Trade Union movement I've never come across conditions like those in the contract cleaning business. It's like something out of the nineteenth century.'
>
> John Vickers, General Secretary, Civil Service Union

Recently women have increasingly organized their own groups within the unions. They have formed what are known as action groups, in which women go on strike as a group but join a large union for support. An example of this is the night cleaners, who became part of the Transport and General Workers Union. They are in a particularly weak position: they are 'invisible workers', cleaning office blocks while everyone else is asleep, in isolation from each other and at the mercy of their employers. They are employed by contractors, large companies who undertake the cleaning of offices for huge profits. May Hobbs, who led the Cleaners' Action Group, describes the work and her experience of the Union (our italics):

First of all, all the night cleaners are women who cannot do day work, because they have families. There are not many intellectual night jobs around, such as office work, so the *only job available* to these women is night cleaning. The big firms of cleaning contractors also found they could get more work done and *make a bigger profit* by employing women at night.

They can exploit these women for the simple reason that *they need the money*. They don't do night jobs for the benefit of their health or because they want to get away from their husbands and children. They go out to work because they need the money desperately – *for little luxuries* like food, rent and clothes for their kids. The cleaning contractors like to tell you a different story – that the cleaners work for holidays and colour televisions. Well I suppose that's true, if you want to look at it like that – but it's holidays and colour televisions for the contractors' families – not for the cleaners themselves! Who are the people who do night cleaning? Some of the women are one-parent unsupported families. Also you have a minority of older women of 40 to 50, but the majority of night cleaners are 20 to 30, *all with young families*, and their husbands tend to be in the lower-paid jobs.

When I first started up in night cleaning I was getting £9 a week. The average wage now, twelve and a half years later, is still only £14 a week, so it hasn't gone up very much has it? The ones who get the big money – and it's ridiculous to call it that – are only getting £19 a week. But it seems like big money compared to those of us only getting £12 to £14.50 a week. Those getting more have only managed to get that because they went out on strike for it. Joining the union and forming the Cleaners' Action Group is the only way to keep your money up.

"I'M SICK OF WORKING FOR LUXURIES"

People *tend to forget the cleaners*, it's a casual job – everyone assumes that every woman should know how to clean. Every woman *does* know how to clean, but they don't have to clean a great big office block. You need training to use the machines for office cleaning – *it's a bloody sight harder than housework!* The office workers aren't the cleanest people in the world. They slop their tea and coffee in the waste bins while the actual waste paper's usually at the side of the bin, so you have to crawl on your hands and knees to get that straightened out. The average office cleaner does about fifty to sixty offices per night. For that they have to empty all the waste-paper bins, around 300–400, sweep all the offices, then you have to hoover, you have to dust, you have to clean the toilets, lifts, then the back stairs, then the front stairs. You have to do all that in an eight-hour shift and if you don't get it done then you have to stay until you do. And because these women need the money so desperately *they will bow to anything* and that is the reason that you have to have this industry organized.

When the night cleaners came out, we got no help from the union. Women must learn to use the union to form an action group – otherwise the union will ignore you. You must use it as an umbrella. You must be in the union and then make your own decisions and tell the union bosses. Get the rank and file behind you – they are the best, but they will only support you in a union. At one strike we just told the union official to get lost because he was doing no good for us, we were getting no support or strike pay. *Women are backward in coming forward* – content to be union officers, but not general secretary.

Women only get militant when they are under stress – but they should be militant all the time.

Women in action – the background to the night cleaners' campaign

The victimization of one cleaner, who was a union member, led to their first strike in April 1971. They realized that the same victimization could happen to any one of them. These are some of the problems that confronted them:

Supervisors were against any union members because they might 'cause trouble'. Therefore many women were reluctant to join for fear of losing their jobs. Immigrant women, who may not have been familiar with their rights, were particularly afraid to join.

More union members were needed. They needed fifty members before they could form their own branch of the Transport and General Workers Union.

Recruiting people was hard. Cleaners rush into work at 10 p.m. and they don't have time to talk.

The union itself. After paying their dues for months the cleaners found the union wouldn't negotiate because there wasn't what they considered enough support. They wanted half the cleaners in any building to join before they would negotiate rates.

The officials were very hard to pin down. One official, who was responsible for the cleaners, passed on the information that the contractors refused the request to have windows open, because it was well known that women were hysterical, and they MIGHT THROW THEMSELVES OUT.

It was very hard to get meetings organized. Women came from all parts of London. They could only attend at weekends and that meant getting babysitters.

Many women had been told that unions were responsible for rising prices and so they were against them.

In spite of these difficulties, a strike was held, with successive strikes at other buildings, until their demands, or some of them, were met. These were the demands:

THE CLEANERS ACTION GROUP DEMAND
£18.75 per week wages.
Sick pay.
Two weeks' pay instead of notice, or two weeks' notice in writing.
Holiday pay – one day for every month worked.
Adequate staffing on all buildings.
Adequate cover money.
Recognition of Union.

Night cleaners want more pay, but there are also other

demands which relate to general conditions. Until we are stronger our best bet is through the Fair Wages resolution.

LOCAL DEMANDS
Conditions vary from building to building. Direct bargaining, e.g. over ventilation, the length of breaks, could be effective, if there is support from other buildings cleaned by the same contractor.

TRANSPORT
At present, many of the women travel long distances to work in London. Many live in south, east or north-east London and have to get to the City or the West End. In Lancaster the cleaners have won the right of free transport to work. Why not in London?

CONTROL
Any increase in wages is nearly always accompanied by a reduction of the women employed on a building. So the women pay back their increase by doing more work. Cleaners should be able to see the contract, and the union should be able to keep a check on the numbers employed to make sure the employers are not fiddling numbers.

PROTECTION AND RESTRICTION
Women can't afford to be against protective legislation in general because at present women are doing two jobs. We should try to get protective legislation extended to men so that it can't be used as an excuse to pay women less.
At present, the difference between male and female rates in cleaning is justified on the grounds that women are not required to stretch to do high-level work.

EQUIPMENT
Cleaning contractors should provide more equipment.

Cleaners now get about £14.50 in London. Since the first action, cleaners in other places have become more militant. This campaign was based on very determined effort, by a strong action group of women, who had against them the employers, their own supervisors, their own union and some of the women cleaners themselves.

Fakenham – 'A silly lot of girls'

There are other examples of action by women. At Fakenham in Norfolk, women workers were suddenly given notice to quit by their bosses. Instead, they took over their leather goods factory and kept it going, getting help from other unions and taking orders and running the business in a collective way. Edna Roach, one of the Fakenham women, makes this point about women and the unions: 'The one big thing workers in industry can learn is not to do what we did – just take things as they were – but to become more involved in unions. It's a big mistake for women to sit on the sidelines and I'm afraid they all too often have. We learned this lesson the very hard way.'

Another woman adds: 'The union officials told us to go home and not be a silly lot of girls. They expected us to be out of here in a week.'

Nancy McGrath makes the same point as May Hobbs: 'I don't think a women's union would get the overall membership, they'll never get the funds to support any sort of dispute. I think what they have to do is to remain in the unions that they have and get them restructured from the bottom up.'

In 1968 1,000 Ford machinists went on strike asking for the same rate of pay as the men – and with the men's support. In 1970 Leeds clothing workers went on strike because their rise was lower than the men's. There are many other examples of women who have taken action and been successful. There is not much that women can do to change things individually but, as they have shown, you are much stronger once you are organized.

So, if you are ever in a job where you want to get a union organized, these are the steps to be taken:

(1) Hold regular meetings and enrol new members.
(2) Organize discussions and invite speakers.
(3) Take up matters of discrimination against women.
(4) Get equal pay talks going.
(5) Get members going to local branch meetings.

What sort of things at work would make you feel dissatisfied or would you want changed? What would you do?

Does your father complain about his work conditions? Does your mother? Has your father ever been involved in a strike or an industrial dispute? Has your mother?

Equal pay and anti-discrimination

> **Male manual worker – 71.8p per hour for 48.5 hour week.**
> **Female manual worker – 49.8p per hour for 40.7 hour week.**
>
> from LEONORA LLOYD, *Women Workers in Britain*,
> Socialist Women Publications

THE EQUAL PAY ACT

What are the main issues that the unions are concerned with? At the moment, the Equal Pay Act has been introduced, aimed at having women's wages equal to men's from 1 January 1975. This is seen as a great advance in women's work situation, but on its own it will not bring real equality in work and wages to women. For example:

(1) It does not give equal pay to women doing 'women's' work where there are no men doing the same type of work.

(2) It does not stop employers from discriminating against women through 'job evaluation' studies. This means working

out how much payment each job deserves. If they base their studies on the physical strength required, men will always be found the most highly graded jobs.

(3) Even if trade unions make an agreement with their employers, it does not have to be extended to women.

(4) The penalties for breaking the laws are mild and unlikely to deter employers from ignoring the Act.

Women have always been a reserve of cheap labour for employers – it will take more than an Equal Pay Act to radically change the role of women in the labour market.

THE ANTI-DISCRIMINATION BILL

This means that it will be illegal to discriminate against a person on the grounds of their sex, i.e. to refuse a job, training or promotion because of the sex of the applicant. While this is a step in the right direction as far as women are concerned, it will not be a final answer. Because of certain exceptions, there will be loopholes for employers:

– where the nature of the job requires it to be performed by a woman (or man) (e.g. foster-mother);

– where a woman (or man) is needed for authenticity (e.g. acting);

– where a mixed team is needed for social work or education (e.g. probation officers);

– employment in single-sex institutions (e.g. convent);

– where communal living accommodation is essential (e.g. ships);

– where it would be offensive to 'public taste or decency' for a woman (or man) to do the job (no example is given for this – lavatory cleaners, perhaps?);

– where customers' preferences make it essential to employ a woman (or man) (again, no example is given; hostesses may be an example).

Examine these exceptions – do you think they are all necessary and justified? The one thing the Bill does not cover, however, is discrimination in education, which leads to lack of equal opportunity. This is a vital omission.

Any laws passed dealing with discrimination and equal pay have to be very detailed and comprehensive – otherwise there will be loopholes. The Equal Opportunities Commission has been set up to investigate the workings of these laws. However, at the moment its powers are very limited.

Here is one example of recent action by women over their work situations. This Charter was drawn up by a group of trade unionists called the London Trades Council, and has been adopted by other unions and groups. These groups are taking up the demands that women workers are making.

LONDON TRADES COUNCIL
WORKING WOMEN'S CHARTER

We pledge ourselves to agitate and organize to achieve the following aims:

(1) The rate for the job, regardless of sex, at rates negotiated by the trade unions, with a national minimum wage below which no wages should fall.

(2) Equal opportunity of entry into occupations and in promotion, regardless of sex and marital state.

(3) Equal education and training for all occupations and compulstory day-release for all 16- to 19-year-olds in employment.

(4) Working conditions to be, without deterioration of previous conditions, the same for women as for men.

(5) The removal of all legal and bureaucratic impediments to equality, e.g. with regard to tenancies, mortgages, pension schemes, taxation, passports, control over children, social security payments, hire-purchase agreements.

(6) Improved provision of local authority day nurseries, free of charge, with extended hours to suit working mothers; provision of nursery classes in day nurseries; more nursery schools.

(7) 18 weeks' maternity leave with full nett pay before and after the birth of a live child; 7 weeks after birth if the child is stillborn. No dismissal during pregnancy or maternity leave. No loss of security, pension or promotion prospects.

(8) Family planning clinics supplying free contraception to be extended to cover every locality. Free abortion to be readily available.

(9) Family allowances to be increased to £2.50 per child, including the first child.

(10) To campaign among women to take an active part in the trade unions and in political life so that they may exercise influence commensurate with their numbers and to campaign among men trade unionists that they may work to achieve this aim.

It will be interesting to see how far they get. For at the moment, in the words of the official government report on discrimination:

'We have a situation of inequality between men and women, in which women generally are the losers. As a result of tradition, prejudice, social conditioning and market forces, women are at the bottom of the pile in almost every occupation they enter.'

Should women form unions of their own, completely separate from men, in order to avoid being overruled by male trade union officials?

What issues have women gone on strike over? Are they different from the issues that men usually strike over?

How will the Equal Pay Act and the Anti-Discrimination Bill affect your job?

How would you know if you were being discriminated against because of your sex (e.g. at an interview for a job or promotion)? What would you do about it?

What would you do if you found you were being paid less than the opposite sex for doing the same job?

Myths and legends

There are some popular excuses and arguments employers use against taking on women, particularly married women. These are based not on truth but on popular myth.

MYTHS . . . MYTHS . . . MYTHS . . . MYTHS . . . MYTHS

---

(1) Women will inevitably leave to have babies.
(2) They will be continually absent on account of their children's illnesses.
(3) They will be continually absent on account of their husbands' illnesses.
(4) They will not want to do extra work in the evenings.
(5) Women are absent more frequently than men.
(6) Women's turnover rate is higher than men's.
(7) Women work only for 'pin money'.
(8) Women don't mind monotonous, boring jobs.
(9) Women can't do heavy work.

FACTS . . . FACTS . . . FACTS . . . FACTS . . . FACTS

---

(1) Not all women have babies.
(2) Not all women who have babies leave their jobs. If maternity leave were better, fewer still would do so.

(3) For top jobs, few people reach their peak before forty. Few women start families after forty.

(4) Unskilled workers of BOTH sexes have a higher absentee rate than skilled or professional ones. It is the monotony of the job, not the sex of the worker, that is the determining factor.

(5) Turnover rate also applies to unskilled workers, who have no responsibility to keep them in their jobs. Firms who have introduced training schemes for semi-skilled women have greatly reduced their labour turnover.

(6) If there were greater equality of responsibility in the home, women would be no more absent than men on account of their children.

(7) Most women need the money they earn for essentials.

(8) Women 'put up with' boring jobs because of this necessity – they don't often have the chance to 'choose' to do them.

(9) Many women's jobs are heavy – ever noticed nurses carrying equipment?

FOLLOW UP
AND BIBLIOGRAPHY

If you are interested in finding out more about any of the issues raised in this book, the following sources may be useful:

The Women's Liberation Workshop in London will provide information over the telephone and has a wide range of books and pamphlets for sale at their office, 38 Earlham Street, London WC2, telephone 01-836 6081. They will also be able to give you information about the many other women's centres, groups and organizations which exist throughout Britain.

Things to read

Spare Rib is published monthly from 9 Newburgh Street, London W1, and is also available from most newsagents; also try to get copies of *Women's Voice, Shrew, Power of Women, Women's Report, Red Rag, Women Now* – you can get details of these and many more from the Women's Liberation Workshop or your local women's centre.

Bibliography

Further information and useful addresses can be found in Anna Coote and Tess Gill, *Women's Rights: A Practical Guide*, Penguin, 1974. A comprehensive bibliography is in Sheila Rowbotham, *Women's Liberation and Revolution*, Falling Wall

Press, 1973, available from the Women's Liberation Workshop.

Of general interest

Sandra Allen, Lee Sanders and Jan Wallis (Eds.), *Conditions of Illusion*, Feminist Books, 1974

Simone de Beauvoir, *The Second Sex*, Penguin, 1972

Lee Comer, *Wedlocked Women*, Feminist Books, 1974

Betty Friedan, *The Feminine Mystique*, Penguin, 1963

Hannah Gavron, *The Captive Wife*, Penguin, 1969

Germaine Greer, *The Female Eunuch*, Paladin, 1971

Juliet Mitchell, *Women's Estate*, Pelican, 1973

Elaine Morgan, *The Descent of Woman*, Corgi, 1974

Robin Morgan (Ed.), *Sisterhood is Powerful*, Vintage Books (U.S.), 1970

Sheila Rowbotham, *Woman's Consciousness, Man's World*, Penguin, 1974

Micheline Wandor (Ed.), *The Body Politic*, Stage 1, 1972

Fay Weldon, *Down Among the Women*, Penguin, 1973

Virginia Woolf, *A Room of One's Own*, Penguin, 1970

Particularly relevant to this book

The *Equal Pay Act* and the *Anti-Discrimination Bill*: copies can be obtained from H.M.S.O.

Mariarosa Dalla Costa and Selma James, *The Power and Subversion of the Community*, Falling Wall Press, 1972

May Hobbs, *Born to Struggle*, Quartet, 1973

Polly Toynbee, *A Working Life*, Penguin, 1973

Organizations of interest

Women in Education, 63 Clyde Road, Didsbury, Manchester 20.

The Children's Literature Collective, 22 Stanmore Road, Leeds 4.

CISSY (Campaign to Impede Sex Stereotyping in the Young), 24 Cressida Road, London N19.

Children's Books Study Group, 42 Kynaston Road, London N16.

The Sex Discrimination Campaign, National Co-ordinator, 148 Bushey Mill Lane, Watford, Herts.

The Trades Union Congress, Great Russell Street, London WC1, telephone 01-636 4030, will give you information about how to join a union.

Films about women and work

Betteshanger, Kent 1972 (10 mins., black and white, £3.00). About a woman involved in organizing other women in a Kent mining community to support the 1972 miners' strike.

Women of the Rhondda (20 mins., black and white, £4.50). This film is based on interviews with four women about their memories of the General Strike and the role of women in mining communities in the 1920s and 1930s.

Fakenham Occupation (10 mins., black and white, £3.00). This film is about the takeover of a shoe factory by women workers threatened with redundancies.

Blow for Blow (*Coup pour Coup*) (90 mins., colour, £20.00,). A fictional account of the successful takeover of a textile factory by a group of women workers. This film is based on a number of factory takeovers in France over the last few years in which women were particularly active. It has had such an impact in France that factory owners have felt the need to agitate against its showing.

(These films are available from The Other Cinema, 12/13 Little Newport Street, London WC2, telephone 01-734 8508.)